Selected works by Fred Wah

Among. Toronto: Coach House Press, 1972.

Earth. Canton, N.Y.: Institute of Further Studies, 1974.

Pictograms from the Interior of BC. Vancouver: Talonbooks, 1980.

Loki is Buried at Smoky Creek: Selected Poetry. Vancouver: Talonbooks, 1980.

Breathin' My Name With a Sigh. Vancouver: Talonbooks, 1981.

Waiting for Saskatchewan. Winnipeg: Turnstone Press, 1985.

Music at the Heart of Thinking. Red Deer: Red Deer College Press, 1987.

So Far. Vancouver: Talonbooks, 1991.

Alley Alley Home Free. Red Deer: Red Deer College Press, 1992.

Diamond Grill. Edmonton: NeWest Press, 1996.

Titles in the Writer as Critic Series
edited by Smaro Kamboureli

VI:Readings from the Labyrinth
Daphne Marlatt
ISBN 1-896300-34-0; $18.95pb

V; Nothing But Brush Strokes: Selected Prose
Phyllis Webb
ISBN 0-920897-89-4; $17.95pb

IV: Canadian Literary Power
Frank Davey
0-920897-57-6; $17.95pb

III: Invisible Ink: crypto-frictions
Aritha van Herk
ISBN 0-920897-07-X; $14.95

II: Signature Event Cantext
Stephen Scobie
ISBN: 0-920897-68-1; $12.95pb

I: Imaginary Hand
George Bowering
ISBN 0-920897-52-5; $12.95pb

Faking It

Poetics and Hybridity

Critical Writing 1984–1999

FRED WAH

THE WRITER AS CRITIC: VII
General Editor
Smaro Kamboureli

NeWest Press

Canadian Cataloguing in Publication Data
Wah, Fred, 1939-
Faking it

(Writer as critic series ; 7)
ISBN 1-896300-07-3

1. Poetics. I. Title. II. Series.
PN1042.W34 2000 808.1 C00-910226-4

Editor for the Press: Smaro Kamboureli
Cover design: Brenda Burgess
Author photograph: Don Denton

The author wishes to thank the following writers and publishers for permission to quote from their publications: Rae Armantrout, Marie Annharte Baker, George Bowering, Di Brandt, Marilyn Dumont, Sherril Grace, Claire Harris, Lyn Hejinian, Yunte Huang, the Estate of Roy Kiyooka, Myrna Kostash, Yasmin Ladha, Daphne Marlett, Stever McCaffery, Scott McFarlane, Roy Miki, Harryette Mullen, Ellie Nichol for bpNichol, Rajinderpal Pal, Nancy Shaw, Ron Silliman, Brian Kim Stefans, Shelley Wong, Third Woman Press for Theresa Hak Kyung Cha, and Xerxes Irani for his "When I was eight" font. Every effort has been made to obtain permission for quoted materials. If there is an omission or error the author and publisher would be grateful to be so informed.

The Canada Council for the Arts since 1957 | Le Conseil des Arts du Canada depuis 1957

Committed to the development of culture and the arts | Alberta Lotteries | The Alberta Foundation for the Arts | Alberta

NeWest Press acknowledges the support of the Canada Council for the Arts for our publishing program. We also acknowledge the financial support of the Government of Canada through the Book Publishing Industry Development Program (BPIDP) for our publishing activities.

NeWest Publishers Limited
Suite 201, 8540–109 Street
Edmonton, Alberta T6G 1E6
(780) 432–9427

1 2 3 4 5 04 03 02 01 00

PRINTED AND BOUND IN CANADA

for Pauline

on the road and at the table
love the talk that books enable

Contents

Contexts and Acknowledgements

I've always enjoyed writing poetry as a way of reading and thinking. The act of critically thinking has for me been more one of exploration and discovery. I think of the essay in the sense of something one tries out, or on. That's why the language and methods of poetry have always seemed right to me; they push at the boundaries of thinking; they play in the noise and excess of language; they upset and they surprise. To write critically I've always written poetry.

So, I feel, I have to "fake it" a little to claim space in this Writer as Critic series. I admit to a certain pretense in the formal essay because I find it a struggle to let logic and argument have control. For a variety of reasons, social and cultural, I want to undercut the hegemony of such forms.

The "Strangle" pieces here serve some of that desire to intervent and push at the boundaries of more intentional compositions. They are, to an extent, sealed from easy understanding in order to play out the possible and sustaining blur around book reviews and other gestures like the critical biotext "Was Eight." I've used these sections as a way of keeping open my own thinking, by play, dissonance, and juxtaposition.

As a poet who's never trusted meaning and its prior constructions, I also find it necessary and useful to sometimes fake language. This action is not so much fraudulent as generative.

I find I need to make things up for myself, or I want to camouflage the critical gaze to gain some loft and, hopefully, new perspective. In one essay, for example, I wanted to twist "feminist" into "feminant" to trouble the predictable and variously constructed meanings that "feminist" has come to carry. I didn't, though, because sometimes it seems easier to not have to explain things. I grew up in an unaccented "cafe." Words like "diapause" (between) and "metapole" (between the eyes) usefully offer themselves from dictionary distillation. "Transing" has become an important compound in my poetics of writing actions that have to do with translation, transcreation, transposition, i.e., senses of crossing, and shifting. My linguistic terminology is grounded in the descriptive linguistics I studied in the sixties with Henry Lee Smith, Jr. The reader can find terms like "micromorphemes" and "suprasegmentals" in Smith's and others' texts of that time.

The writing in this book is from 1984 to 1999. Most of it was written during some major shifts in cultural production and critical thinking. Poetry itself, particularly in the US, has registered significant alterations in a move from speech-based or process poetics to a more socially formative response. Cultural politics have fluctuated dramatically in North America as multiculturalism has troubled the status quo. Critical discourse and theory have been lush with postmodern surprise and insight. Many boundaries are being crossed in interdisciplinary and creative projects. Preparing this collection presented me with my own angst over much of this change in the last part of this century.

The writing in this book is a mixture of forms: essay,

interview, review, poem, letter, journal. Though I've tried not to repeat myself, I find that I keep saying many things over and over. This is partly due to lapses in time between comments that either become qualified by new thinking or to the repetition of fundamental ideas.

"Faking It" was presented at "Inglish: Writing With An Accent," a *West Coast Line* conference in Vancouver, November 20, 1992, and published in *West Coast Line* the following year. Some of this piece was sluiced out for my biofiction, *Diamond Grill.*

In the eighties I wrote two papers that loosely collated the poetics of "estrangement" I had come to understand as the generative function of the kind of poetry I'm interested in and the kind of poetry that might effect social reconstruction. "Making Strange Poetics" was presented at the "Long-liners" conference on the long poem at York University in 1984. "Making Stranger Poetics" was written for a Canadian studies conference in Australia in 1990 and the subtitle of my presentation was "A Canadian Poetics (Plural) Inventory." Both papers worked loosely around the notion of estrangement in what now seems a rather naive negotiation between a poetics of process and a more current critique of language as social form. I've spliced, or strang(l)ed, the two papers here as a way of grounding some of the terms, thinking that, despite their unstable epistemological status, they still seem worth keeping in the poetics toolbox.

I wrote "A Poetics of Ethnicity" for the Canadian Studies Conference, "Twenty Years of Multiculturalism: Successes and Failures," February 28–March 2, 1991, St. John's College, University of Manitoba. It was included in the published proceedings, *Twenty Years of Multiculturalism: Successes and Failures*. I was then just coming to the discourses of multicultural, racialized, and ethnic writing and, without too much concern for differences between those terms, wanted to locate for myself, in the context of an official Canadian multiculturalism, the terms of a writing that had been marginalized by continued attempts to homogenize CanLit.

"Half-Bred Poetics" is a paper I presented at the Association for the Study of New Literatures in English (Germany, July 2, 1994). An address to "hybridity" as a particular dynamic in the conflagrations around racialized writing, it was written just prior to the controversial "Writing Thru Race" conference in Vancouver. I regretted that, by accepting the invitation to present in Germany, I would miss "Writing Thru Race." But I also felt some pleasure at having the opportunity to claim a space for the particular poetics of racialized writing with which I felt aligned, in a "new" literature still being constructed within the "old" world. At the same time I felt conflicted about my own posturing on what some were essentializing as "the racial bandwagon"; I was and am certainly "on" it but I want to exercise the particularity of being in-between (as well as being outside-of). Hybridity in writing is realized as a more complicated possibility in a later piece, "Speak My Language."

The "Interview with Ashok Mathur" was conducted over email and published by Ashok on his website and in *filling Station*. I've found it to be a very useful interview to pass on to inquisitive students writing term papers on *Diamond Grill*.

"Speak My Language: Racing the Lyric Poetic" was written for and presented at the Cross-Cultural Poetics Conference at the University of Minnesota, October 16–19, 1997. The panel was on Canadian multiculturalism and included papers by Roy Miki and Jeff Derksen. Roy published our three papers in *West Coast Line* (24). Over the past couple of years, the dilemma of gearing a poetics for social change in racial awareness has continued to confront writers of race. The complicity with narrative form in the "mainstream" novel is particularly complicated by the capitalization of "multiculturalism." Poetry can, to a certain extent, still offer possibilities of formal intervention since its consumption does not seriously offer much economic profit. I believe my main point remains, however, as this text suggests, that the race writer can be suspicious of any previously constructed poetics. The consequences of such dubitable inducements might, happily, lead a Cha, a Mullen, or an Ismail to intersect her own predicates and articulate a more liquid and multiple *ethnos* for an uncaged lyric.

"Chinese Avant-Garde Poetry" is made up of notes for a talk I gave to the Asian Studies Group at the University of Calgary in November 1996. In my preparatory reading for my trip to China earlier that year, I was curious about the mediation implied when a term like "avant-garde" is used by both Chinese and American literary scholars to describe recent

Chinese poetry. As well, the talk was intended to offer a brief "report" on a "cultural exchange" trip to China that summer.

"Objects of Resistance: An Interview with Hong Kong poet Leung Ping-Kwan" was originally published in a special issue of *West Coast Line* (21 [30/3] Winter 1996–97) as "Transporting the Emporium: Hong Kong Art and Writing Through the Ends of Time." I interviewed Leung at the end of my China trip, on September 1, 1996. The interview was useful as a measure of some of the self-consciousness I had experienced on the mainland. P.K.'s comprehension of the "Chinese" poetic scene, because of his more crucial international intersection, seems, just prior to Hong Kong's reversion to Chinese rule, a highly aware consideration, both about the ways in which Hong Kong fits into the picture as well as about the colonial and island dynamics of trying to write poetry in the late twentieth century. Besides *City at the End of Time* (1992), his most recent books are *Poetry of Moving Signs* (1994) and *Museum Pieces* (1996).

In the summer of 1996 I made a three-week trip to China as a member of a small group of Canadian artists on a government-funded cultural exchange. I was interested in meeting as many contemporary Chinese poets as I could and was guided principally by a publication I had noticed a few years earlier, *Original: Chinese Language-Poetry Group*, and by help from Yunte Huang in Buffalo and Tim Lilburn in Saskatoon. I had some names. I was keen to hear "their side of the story." Since Tiananmen, there have been an increasing number of translations of contemporary Chinese poetry based, I believe, mostly on a kind of current western Orientalism that seeks cultural inhabitation by globalization. I was interested to talk with these poets about how they see themselves in such a context. The essay "Chinese Avant-Garde Poetry" has been put together from notes for a talk I gave at the University of Calgary upon my return. The interview with Leung Ping-Kwan was done on that same trip and I transcribed it for a special issue of *West Coast Line* on Hong Kong. The first portion of "China Journal" was published in *Displace* (1, 1997) and then in *Prairie Fire* (18/4, Winter 1997–98). This fuller version was published in *Xcp Cross Cultural Poetics* (3, 1998). As it stands, this journal could still be extended to include later trips to Taiwan and Singapore where I had the opportunity to question poets about the globalization of literature.

"Poetics of the Potent" is a slightly revised version of what appeared in a special issue of *Open Letter* (9/2, Spring 1995) edited by Susan Rudy. It was originally presented at the Indian Association of Canadian Studies Conference at Gujarat University in Ahmedabad, January 6–9, 1992.

"bp's Last Notebook" was written for a panel presentation at "On the Horizon: bpNichol after Ten," a *West Coast Line* event at Emily Carr College of Art and Design in Vancouver in September 1998. This improvisatory critical "cataloguing" of bp's last notebook engaged me not only as a means to discriminate certain of his compositional approaches but also as a means to locate part of a relationship with a very close friend. I had spent a few weeks in July 1988 teaching with beep at the Red Deer College writers' workshop so I was interested to coordinate in my mind some of the conversation we had had that summer with the writing he was doing in his journal. Ellie Nichol found the notebook, several years after beep's death, fallen behind some furniture, and I was with Roy Miki in Toronto when she asked him to rejoin it to the rest of bp's papers in the SFU collection. It's a wonderfully active notebook, as all of his are, and on seeing it I felt drawn to the "action" in it and invited by its intensity to doodle, further.

"Dear Hank" is a kind of epistolary journal I wrote to Hank Lazer in the spring of 1999. During a trip to Southeast Asia I used an essay of Hank's on Ron Silliman to triangulate some thinking around the language of travel and tourism. My letter/journal ponders my own position as a tourist through reading several texts. Hank's essay considers two volumes of Ron Silliman's multi-volume project, *The Alphabet: What* (1988) and *Xing* (1966). I refer to a short selection from another volume of *The Alphabet, You*, published in a recent issue of *CrossConnect*. Silliman's *The Alphabet* is a project he began in 1980. By 1999 he had completed about twenty of the projected twenty-six books. Hank Lazer has published widely in both poetry and criticism. *Opposing Poetries*, his two-volume examination and reading of L=A=N=G=U=A=G=E poetry and poetics, is an important source for understanding this radical shift in cultural poetics.

"Loose Change (A Molecular Poetics)" was originally published by Louis Cabri in *Hole* (6, 1996). It is, in part, an extension of thoughts that came up in "Poetics of the Potent" relating to the "particles" in writing that can become dynamic when attention is paid to the particular. In conversation, Louis has talked of "below the word poetics," a poetry that considers the sub-word "fragment" in its political and social implications. So, this paper overlaps with his concern to locate language's shadow (detritus, static, noise, etc.) as a productive arena for poetry.

Smaro Kamboureli has been an inspiring and extremely supportive editor for this book. She nudged me into it several years ago and I'm sure without her I would have happily let it compost away. I have learned from her sharp eye for economy and form, and her intelligence and love of poetry and thought have really shaped this book. Pauline Butling is more than a companion and friend; together we've shared our books and had many years of kitchen table talk and long journey discussions about writing and reading. I think her own imagination informs my writing as much as my own sometimes, as well as her astute editor's eye. Many students and friends over the years have offered their community. Roy Miki is a sympathetic partner and we share a great deal of our interest in racialized writing and in poetry; his piloting of *West Coast Line* was crucial for contemporary poetics. I have been Jeff Derksen's teacher and student for longer than it has taken to write this book. Frank Davey has provided generous accommodation over many years with *Open Letter*. Colleagues Jeanne Perreault, Susan Rudy, Aritha van Herk, and Nicole Markotic not only show up at the readings but afford necessary dialogue and community. Louis Cabri's and Ashok Mathur's interests and publishing smarts continue to provide direction.

I'd like to thank all of my graduate and writing students at the University of Calgary for giving me the privilege of learning from their reading and writing.

My department at the University of Calgary has been generous in its support for attending many of the conferences at which these papers were presented. The Calgary Institute for the Humanities was the first home for this project when I was a fellow there a few years ago. An artist's residency at the Banff Centre for the Arts provided further habitation for this work.

Faking It

All that language in the cafes (those brown-skinned men pinch me and talk in Chinese not to me but to the mysterious gutteral nine-toned air by the big maple chopping block in the kitchen) and then hear my father speak from out of his/our mouth these same words with an axe to the edge of them, him with command and authority because he's smart, he's the boss, and he can scorn their playfulness, their naiveté, because his mouth can move with dexterity between these men-sounds, between these secret sounds we only hear in the kitchen of the Elite or in the silent smoke-filled Chinese store, between these dense vocables of nonsense, and English, which was everywhere, at the front of the cafe, on the street, and at home. And that he did this alone, that no one else could move between these two tongues like he did, that put him at the centre of our life, with more pivot to the world than anyone I knew.

At home the English was my mother love with laughing and *Just Mary* on CBC and big red volumes of *Journeys Through Bookland* and at supper when we'd see him he might make a little slip of tongue, an accent which we would think twice about correcting and at least a quick glance before laughing at, sometimes with him, but watch out for his quick dagger defence, "You smart-aleck kids, you think you know so much, you don't know anything, you go to school but you're not so high muckamuck," and that'd be the redness in his face, the English problem, him exposed.

Sometimes my mother's parents spoke a little Swedish in front of me but they didn't speak much except to argue, and my mother had been to school so she spoke only English. She said finally she could understand the Swedish but could no longer speak it. She had been half-erased by the time she met my dad and her English was good, it was blonde.

My father joined the Lions Club in Nelson. The Lions Club is one of those "service" clubs like the Rotary Club. We also had the Gyros and the JCs; JC stood for Junior Chamber of Commerce, I think. And that's what most of the clubs were for, business connections, working on community projects, and having some fun. Most of the clubs met at the Hume Hotel for lunch or dinner once a week and each meeting was full of shenanigans, like having to pay a fine for not wearing a tie and things like that. My dad really enjoyed the Lions Club and he worked hard on projects for the club, like coaching Little League baseball and putting on the mid-summer bonspiel pancake breakfast on Baker Street. I think what he enjoyed most, though, was the kidding around. Some of the old guys in town still say to me, "Your dad was quite a kidder."

I think a lot of his kidding around was in order to hide his embarrassment at not knowing English as well as he'd have liked to. His only schooling in English he picked up during six months in Cabri, Saskatchewan, just north of Swift Current. His father sent him there to work in a small cafe when he first came back from China. And then one of his sisters, Hanna, helped him out with reading and writing a bit during those first years back with his English-speaking family. Whatever else he learned about English he picked up from working in the cafe. So, when he joined the Lions Club and had to give an initiation speech, he had my mother help him write something up. She says he was very nervous about this event, worried that he might flub it, make a fool of himself, the only Chinaman at an all-white dinner meeting. So there he was, with his little speech on a piece of paper in front of all these Baker St. nickel millionaires in the Hume Hotel dining room, thanking these guys for inviting him to join their club, thanking them for making Nelson such a wonderful place to live and raise his family, and then thanking them for this meal with the wonderful "sloup." We always kidded around at home when he said "sloup" and he'd laugh and, we thought, even say it that way intentionally just to horse around with us. But here such a slip just turned him copper red (the colour you get when you mix yellow with either embarrassment or liquor). So when he heard himself say "sloup" for "soup" he stopped suddenly and looked out at the expected embarrassed and patronizing smiles from the crowd. Then he did what he had learned to do so well in such instances, he turned it into a joke, a kind of self-putdown that he knew these white guys liked to hear: he bluffed that Chinamen called soup "sloup" because, as everyone knew, the Chinese made their cafe soup from the slop water in which they washed their underwear and socks, and besides, as everyone also knew, Chinamen liked to"slurp" their soup and make a lot of noise.

So he faked it, and I guess I picked up on that sense of faking it from him, that English could be faked, and I quickly learned that when you fake language you see everything else is a fake.

Amo Amas Amat, Amamus Amatus, Amant. At least that's how I remember it. Miss Darough was my first very British Latin teacher. We were offered French, German, or Latin. The major minority language in school was Russian, the language of the Doukhobors. They had an accent. And no one wanted one. If we learned Latin, we were told, we would learn the basics of English grammar, get the real stuff, from the source, the mother tongue. So I spent a few years, even into the pompous classrooms of Latin at UBC, reading about Caesar's invasion of Britain. We could pretend we were speaking a foreign language, we could imitate what we had been told was the most authentic world view around. It wasn't until years later, when I discovered Louis Zukofsky whitewashing the whole notion of accurate translation, that I could smile about the sham of my synthetic education.

By the time Charles Olson delivered his lectures at Beloit and entitled them "Poetry and Truth," I was committed to the big bamboozle of writing. "You tell the truth the way the words lie," Robert Duncan had admonished us young writers. Olson had performed in Washington, in the American "Space," in our graduate seminars in Buffalo, at his readings everywhere, a rhetoric of public sleight-of-hand. Now you see it, now you don't. Just try to knock old Kronos off the podium, he threatened. Don't play all your cards. His three-hour poetry reading at Berkeley in 1985 outraged his audience as he bobbed and wove through a labyrinth of poetic politics without reading a poem. They thought he was just a buffoon, but back in Buffalo we, his students, praised his braggadocio for showing up the false front of the public poem, for challenging those San Francisco four-flushers' attempt to appropriate the scene. The politics of poetry, at least American poetry, didn't seem, finally, any different from the bluster and fanfare of my Eurocentric teachers.

And when I got back to Canada I ran into fiction. How to fake love in a new land. The tall tale, the anecdote, the fib, the jest—the novel. The stud horse man, indeed. The horse, indeed. Sick and lonely BC Chinaman out looking for the ancestral bones falls in love with an Indian sorceress who is the daughter of an old Chinese cooley. Vancouver's ships cross Rockies. A foothills picara screws every man in sight, without a condom. "What about AIDS?" I said. "It's only fiction," she screams back. And so we smile complicity as the counterfeits and forgeries of the dreamed-of language of paradise lead us on, and deke us, finally, into trusting these "labyrinths of voice."

I had always stumbled through grammar tests and essays in a haze, nearly failing English in my first year at UBC. I faked as best I could, trying to overcome the imprint of accent or just plain ignorance. Who knows? I studied music, which seemed somehow more forgiving as a language, until finally the formalities (again, all European) constrained. Except for jazz, where dissonance and unpredictability are welcomed, where the contrived, the flash, is valued. And except for Warren Tallman who took my wild (and, by then, a little angry) jabs at poetry as serious. I wanted truth and the real, the absolute face of feeling and, above all, a language that wasn't British. Anything in translation, particularly Rilke. So I took to the poem as to jazz, as a way to subvert the authority of the formal, as a way to sluice out "my" own voice for myself.

But the more I wrote the more I discovered that faking it is a continual theatre of necessity. No other way to be in language, but to bluff your way through it, stalling for more time. And when I get it, that little gap of renewal, I see the accent not in my own little voice, but there in the mouth of the word within the word, there in the "land only of what is," right there at the tips of our fingers, in the "sniff" of the pen as it hunts the page.

Strangle One

Why return dispersal's genetic wanting one ethnic thing to show itself in the break-up of a marked body to keep out of sight of the package to trip the diapause of meaning cut the key into accent unexpected tumblers open to the many-forgotten messages hungry for new arrangements punctuated forever by those silent metopoles of breath, just that, breathing.

The fascicle *Earth* and "A Plan for a Curriculum of the Soul." End of the sixties. Back into the mountains, excited about the "crossing over" from the east to the west, from the old to the new (Lawrence's "New Heaven and Earth"), from acid to mushroom (Castaneda's creek leap), from then to now (bpNichol's "Journeying and the Returns"). *Eth* as ethos, home. And ethic. Earth household, and all that. Etcetera. Still a little too much gauze, eh, the national ethnic, that B&B (bilingual and bicultural) left out. Racial hybridity's a process of locating, dis-cerning, writing through identity's fictions by unmarking just enough history that memory's allowed a sometimes quick triple-tongue, just enough speed so that movement's possible. "Your own anthropology jumps like a bear from the apple tree." Camouflage over. Frappe la rue, Fred. "On the way to the hospital she said just keep breathing I hadn't even considered it." That's what sighing says, I said.

To write is to move. Dispersal of a presumed and constructed world. To get back, home (unmarking history so memory can re-cite and re-situate). Then ethic, earth as ethic (discern literally what's there to stand on, "Back to the land," the communal, intrasubjective blip to resist "America"), then, later, the ethnic (that piss-wall of the racial stained, yet zipped eth-ik forward into and along with newly noted difference).

Yet "h$_{om}{}^{om}$e" has become also, in its diasporic recitation, a snatch block that nostalgically anchors and commodifies communal and inherited (acclaimed in the "new" world) imaginaries.

Thought of the *eth* as value. Problem: anything of value will get exchanged, not necessarily changed. That is, the ethnic, in North America, prefigures the bite of race (just like the purity of race, for the hybrid, encloses the hyphen).

I've wanted to see how writing leads itself, as part of the traditional narrative of value, the Quest, El Dorado, Truth, the Other, and so forth. Traditional notions of value—Idealism, Positivism, Moralism—and even the present political, almost-religious value, Economism all cling to value as "right way." Narratives of meaning always include the discontinuous and the fragmentary. The hieroglyphics of this "new" have been so enacted as to be, now, consumable.

My first hit on "ethic" came during a writing project for

a series of fascicles called "A Plan for a Curriculum of the Soul." This was part of Charles Olson's tripartite abstraction of value—the True, Good, and the Beautiful—translated in the Olson Curriculum as Politics, Religion, and Epistemology. I did *Earth* (others did *The Mushroom, Blake, Dream, Bach's Belief,* etc.). This was part of the so-called "speech based" poetics (now being called "process" poetics) spinning out of Olson's *mutbologos*—by word of mouth and extending, through the Institute of Further Studies, a pedagogy intended to address a triple "politics, religion, and epistemology" model.

I had written primarily to senses of geography and landscape, a long poem called *Mountain* and a book called *Lardeau* that had a lot to do with timber cruising and firefighting and place (the mountains of southeastern British Columbia where I grew up). *Music at the Heart of Thinking* is the trajectory of that processing of place and value.

The subjects:

STUMBLING
ANIMALS (imprint)
MAKING STRANGE
NEGATIVE CAPABILITY
SWIMMING (ladder)
SYNCHRONOUS FOREIGNICITY
HUNGER
FAMILY (death, property, bones)
RIVERS AND CREEKS (salmon, salt)
KNOTS (traffic)

TREES (apple, heads of hair)
GRAMMAR
MISTAKE (disgraces are our graces)

To write in poetry is to move past the comfort of a ruled discourse; in order, to move on, beyond order, the complete thought spills over to an excess and residue of language in which my "marked body" dissolves into unsure relationships—remarked.

That sudden catch of breath when the heart rate's almost silent, that little sock of baby breath (not the flower) caught at the end of the gasp. When writing encounters that electrical switch-like gulp for presence it responds to this surprise in minute and cellular behaviour by flowing into the first open path it finds.

Strang(l)ed Poetics

The attention to a ficto-critical, krinopoeic, or theomatic writing is substantially by writers who use formal innovation as a lever into/onto the next word, next step, next act. Action. Their texts animate the boundary condition of writing as exploration and discernment, a liminal picking out for oneself. Strange, stranger, strangled. Writing always seems to encounter the necessary torsion to twist or move across the mass of assumed or inherited condition.

Krinopoeia

Many of us have heard Aritha van Herk's entertaining and performative critical presentations laced with her parodic and quickly thawing story-telling tongue. She has adopted the term "fictocriticism" for this melding of theory and writing, accurate enough to apply to her own critical writing. The term theoms (theory poems) perhaps serves some poetry's interest to engage in the immense wave of postmodern philosophy and theory. In the context of working critically from within poetry, Ezra Pound's foregrounding of the Greek "*KRINO, to pick out for oneself, to choose*" (30) has been a useful naming. George Bowering's *Errata* might thus be "krinopoeic" in that the structure of that text assumes some singular elements of prose paragraph and prose poem composition for reflection and conjecture, ideas and philosophy, values. Other critical/creative gestures have informed my own interest in this twinning. Brian Fawcett's two social ficto-critiques adopt, in part in the name of "creative non-fiction" and in part as pure fiction, the double or reflective interlinear text in William Carlos Williams' *Kora in Hell.* My own ongoing series of poetic texts, *Music at the Heart of Thinking,* was initiated in response to a request from bpNichol to write something on "notation" for *Open Letter,* as was Robert Kroetsch's poem, "The Frankfurt *Hauptbahnhof.*" Kroetsch's own generative poetic essay, "For Play and Entrance: The Contemporary Canadian Long Poem," remains a fulcrum of the fictocritical or poetic essay.

Such writings are instances of, as Charles Bernstein imagines, "poetics as an invasion of the poetic into other realms: overflowing the bounds of genres, spilling into talk, essays, politics, philosophy . . . Poetics as a sort of *applied poetic,* in the sense that engineering is a form of applied mathematics" (1992, 151).

In recent years, feminist poetics have articulated this ficto-critical border crossing in particular ways. *Tessera,* the most significant journal for feminist writing theory in the eighties, brims with investigatory diaries, musings, and wanderings of the *krino:* Nicole Brossard, Daphne Marlatt, Gail Scott, Lola Lemire Tostevin, Yolande Villemaire, France Théoret, Smaro Kamboureli, and many others. For Betsy Warland, for example, the inquisition of the historical imagination leads to what she sees as a "new kind of theory-fiction/theory":

> *No mind and body split, the text embodying the viewing. Form being the frown line above your left brow, the dimple on your right cheek, the word made flesh, the tissue the text (93).*

As a kind of subversion of the *explication du texte,* Erin Mouré includes a section at the back of her poetry book *Furious* entitled "The Acts" (83–101), texts noted and referenced in the poems. The tangible critical plane of the writer reenacting her text: "To take the movement of the eye that is *seeing,* and use it to make the reading surface of the poem" (96).

Even the most significant Canadian long poem, in Canada's short literary history, *The Martyrology,* is seen by its author as dealing "with various perceived splits." And one of these splits, bpNichol tells us, "is to deal with the split between the talking about writing, and writing . . . " (McCaffery "In Ten$^{s}_{t}$ion" 79).

Ostranenie

In Book V of *The Martyrology* the reader is given the choice of reading the poem sequentially as it's laid out or of following alternate reading routes suggested by Nichol through numbered references. We are given some basis for Nichol's interest in estrangement. Book V opens with a quote from Jean Cocteau, "The greatest literary masterpiece is no more than an alphabet in disorder," and a letter from "Matt" which includes the statement: "I had a sudden image of your poetry capturing you like the Minotaur in the labyrinth . . . " Nichol also indicates that Book V is a "gordian knot . . . an untying of the first four books."

This notion of "making strange" is an old one but it has gained currency recently via the oft-quoted 1917 statement by the Russian formalist critic Viktor Shklovsky:

> *And art exists that one may recover the sensation of life; it exists to make one feel things, to make the stone stony. The purpose of art is to impart the sensation of things as they are perceived and not as they are known. The technique of art is to make objects "unfamiliar," to make forms difficult, to increase the difficulty and length of perception because the process of perception is an aesthetic end in itself and must be prolonged. Art is a way of experiencing the artfulness of an object; the object is not important (12).*

Even the varied lexicon of critical desire and possibility shows a continuing need to reinvent/renew perceptions that otherwise might reify: defamiliarization, deconstruction, displacement, negative capability, or nonnarrative, not knowing, indeterminacy, silence, distortion, parataxis, non referentiality, dictation, ambiguity, disfunctioning, fragmentation, undecidability, *Differenzqualität,* departure, derivation, opposition, divergence, alter-native, and on and on.

I use "estrangement" in consideration of the compositional tactic of nonclosure (particularly the sentence and the cadence) in both short and long poems.

For myself, I recognized this poetic first as a heady feeling of release and freedom through Rilke's cries on the cliffs at Duino, Creeley's attack on inherited line structures, Olson's break from the rigid left margin out onto the page, and through my own early years of derivation from these and other nonconventional poets. I was relieved of some educationally instilled guilt and confusion when I read in Fenollosa that the sentence needn't be a complete thought. Robert Duncan's affirmations of aperiodic, noncausal structures kept me intrigued by new and unsuspected possibilities in poetic language. The spine of my copy of Keats' *Selected Letters* is broken open to that letter to his brothers in which he describes the capability "of being in uncertainties, mysteries, doubts, without any irritable reaching after fact and reason . . . " (103). Or perhaps it was during the faltering and strained explorations of one of my first jazz ad libs playing trumpet with the Kampus Kings in 1956. Certainly the jazz model of a freely moving line playing off of and against the bound chord progressions showed me the delight of distortion and surprise.

Prioprioception

Shklovsky's view of art as sensational requires a recognition of the connection between language and the body. Through speech-based poetry of the sixties, sound poetry, free-form music, and through feminist reclamation of the body of and in language, I've found useful and provocative tools that help this recognition.

A line in the "Articulation (sic) Deformation in Play" section of Nicole Brossard's *Daydream Mechanics* (63) strikes me as a good example of how estrangement works at a minute and particular level.

> *river moulded in the calm*
> *flood as fierce and flora fl (63)*

Her perception of the language is so sharp and intense here that she is able to use the root etymon "fl" to jar the poem into the proprioceptive statement she intended by beginning the poem with a reference to "muscle."

•◆•

I picked up "etymon" from seminars by Charles Olson and Henry Lee Smith at Buffalo in the early sixties. I've found it a useful notion not because of recuperative originary "meaning" but more frequently as shift away from expected use, as Brossard does here.

What Steve McCaffery calls "that proprioceptive garbage" (presentation) is that now-problematic notion, forwarded into modern poetics by Olson, that the human is organic. "PROPRIOCEPTION: the data of depth sensibility/the 'body' of us as object which spontaneously or of its own order produces experience of, 'depth' Viz SENSIBILITY WITHIN THE ORGANISM BY MOVEMENT OF ITS OWN TISSUES" (*Additional Prose* 17). I've used Olson's sense of "proprioception" extensively as a means of claiming the physical in writing, though I now realize how troublesome the term is in the face of recent thinking about the body that figures the necessity of a "materialism that questions physicalism" (Grosz 22). I use the term, too easily, perhaps, more as an antidote to preconception and, frequently, as a simple call for spontaneity. I'll let it stand, for now, while I ponder more enlightened clarifications not so much of the "experiencing" subject but of what goes on in writing when we undergo undergoing (Nichols, "Subject" n.p.).

•◆•

For Nicole Brossard the word "body" is aligned to her sense of the terms "writing" and "text." It is, she tells us, "a metaphor for energy, intensity, desire, pleasure, memory, and awareness" ("Corps" 7). Further, "writing is energy taking shape in language." That is, the body takes shape in writing and, if you're a feminist writer, you are obliged to exorcize the patriarchal sememes with "rituals of presence."

> *Let us say that there are two major categories of ritual: ritual with a mask that applies to the story, the novella and the essay, to all writing in prose; and ritual without a mask that particularly concerns poetry. But in one category like the other, there are different practices of ritual: ritual with trembling, ritual with shock, ritual with sliding, and ritual with breath* ("Corps" 10).

There's that "breath" still very central to notions of composition.

•◆•

"Without a mask": the breath of the breath line; breath of the other; "breathing my name with a sigh"; to toke (or fake) enough breath for a long (and musical) phrase. This is practical and applied. See the "Notation" issues of *Open Letter* from the eighties.

•◆•

In a wonderful panel discussion with Daphne Marlatt and George Bowering, bpNichol talks about his sense of how "syntax equals the body structure." He talks about how we emotionally and psychologically armour the body against the limits of such things as low doorways and ceilings.

> *I discovered that the order in which I wrote my poems allows certain contents in and keeps other contents out, i.e., the syntax I choose, the way I tend to structure a piece, form per se, permits some contents and excludes others. So what I was trying to find, because that is part of a larger thing I've been working towards, is a way to increase my own formal range . . . and therefore not merely be stuck, shall we say, by the physical limitation of my body at that point, i.e., just because I'm walking around with my shoulders up like this, if I can learn to relax I can see the world in a slightly different way and so on. If I can keep moving the structure of the poem around, hopefully I can encompass different realities and different ways of looking at things. In that sense, I've always seen a connec-*

> *tion between the breathing I do and what comes out of me, the words I do, so syntax/body structure, sequence/body structure, but also the body of the poem ("Syntax" 25).*

Bowering and Marlatt extend the discussion by talking about the literal physicality of writing with pen and typewriter. Marlatt refers to the "orgasmic feeling" (the much-discussed poetics of closure) in the composition of her long poem *Steveston* in which she feels "the syntax and body and landscape become totally interwoven" (27).

For Erin Mouré the "[i]mage of the whole physical body must always be there. Not truncated, not synecdoche, but the physical image speaking directly the entire body at once" (*Furious* 85).

Gail Scott, struggling with the composition of her novel *Heroine:* "But I can't just sit down and write a novel about X. It all happens in the process of writing. I agree with Barthes that writing has to do with the body pursuing *its own ideas—for my body does not have the same ideas I do*" (*Spaces* 81).

And Daphne Marlatt in "Musing with Mothertongue":

> *the beginning: language, a living body we enter at birth, sustains and contains us. it does not stand in place of anything else, it does not replace the bodies around us. placental, our flat land, our sea, it is both place (where we are situated) and body (that contains us), that body of*

language we speak, our mothertongue. it bears us as we are born in it, into cognition (53).

Long Poem

In order to prolong the moment, and the perceptions available in the delay, the movement, the expectation of movement, must be disturbed and fragmented. In *The Martyrology*, Nichol creates a labyrinthine network of incomplete thought loops in order both to dwell in and explore those loops, as well as to generate the next step forward. That is, he wants to continue, he really doesn't want to stop. He's stopping in order to continue. But the "stopping" cannot be a closure; the disruption, paradoxically, does move the poem forward. Let's follow a few of the links in his chain in Book V. A stanza in link 4:

> this poetry of place & places
> traces of earlier rimes
> out-takes of the muse's movement thru me
> or my own grappling with a wish to speak
> each one a bridge i chose not to take
> reasons lost now in the years between

can be followed by these lines in link 6:

> bridge that flowers
> bridge that is the clicking of my teeth turning
> tongue twisting back on itself

All of which can be shot forward to some concrete visual or sound text in link 11. Through the typically unpredictable vertical hinging by paradigmatic thought suffixes (Levin), Nichol creates an image flux governed only by the speed of thought.

"Paradigmatic thought suffix" is essentially a form of rhyme. Though it can be phonological it is not limited to sound. "Orange—Blue," for example. But it is a "vertical" movement (imagistically, syntactically, semiologically) and, thus, paradigmatic. This is a dynamic in poetic composition that can orient radical networks of thought in reading and writing.

Those structures only get connected because they're placed there. But these vertical relationships can operate beyond the phonological to set up unpredictable strictures for that speeding train of thought: bridge to bridge; bridge to teeth; teeth to tongue twisting; tongue twisting to the sonic visualization of the last letter of a list of seemingly syntactically unconnected words.

Viktor Shklovsky suggests that this arresting of the movement is for the sake of continuity and that this, in fact, constitutes a definition of poetry.

> *In our studies of the lexical and phonetic composition of poetic speech, of word order, and of the semantic structures of poetic speech, we everywhere came upon the same index of the artistic: that it is purposely created to de-automatize the perception, that the goal of its creation is that it be seen, that the artistic is artificially created so*

that perception is arrested in it and attains the greatest possible force and duration, so that the thing is perceived, not spatially, but, so to speak, in its continuity. *These conditions are met by "poetic language . . . " Thus we arrive at the definition of poetry as speech that is braked, distorted (Silliman, "Migratory" 32; emphasis added).*

Just tap the breaks lightly, my father warned when he was teaching me to drive, or else you'll lock them and screech to a complete stop, slide into an oncoming car or ditch, wear them out.

Cadence, and other sites of estrangement

The delayed cadence, as in music, becomes a matter of devising imminent endings out of our desire for rest and conclusion.

In *The Poetics of Indeterminacy,* Marjorie Perloff talks about reading John Ashbery's poem, "These Lacustrine Cities."

Reading Ashbery's text is thus rather like overhearing a conversation in which one catches an occasional word or phrase but cannot make out what the speakers are talking about.

And yet one does keep listening. For the special pleasure of reading a poem like "These Lacustrine Cities" is that disclosure of some

> *special meaning seems perpetually imminent (10–11).*

Ashbery's poem is not a long one but his device of avoiding full recognition at the level of the cadence has become a necessity, particularly to the writer of long poems. The anticipation and imminence beckon. The pleasure of anticipated cadence is a prime factor in Kroetsch's use of the "and . . . but" in *The Sad Phoenician* and of the chain possibilities in Book V of *The Martyrology.* In his presentation at "Long-liners" Nichol noted:

> *one of the things the Concrete Poetry movement taught us as writers was to reclaim the small gesture. some texts need to exist separate from our desire to "collect" them. once we become sensitized to what is happening tonally, imagistically, rhythmically, etc. within the smaller gestural works, we are then in a position to introduce notes with exactly those qualities into a larger composition (13).*

The prosodic matrix in the basic relationship of syllable, line, and cadence is there for the long poem just as it is for the short lyric, but the quality of imminence can become a more outstanding characteristic in the long poem. I fancy Edmond Jabès' *The Book of Questions* as a long poem in which the next line of the text could turn into a novel, for example. But then cadence as an actual ending construct becomes inoperable. The poem, or text (a more suitable term for Jabès' book) can shun its resolution in order to keep going, to stay alive, a common awareness of cadence at the compositional level, as evidenced in a couple of poems. George Bowering's *Kerrisdale Elegies* could, as the poet says, "refuse a closing couplet" (137). Though Bowering is aware of the possibility, he chooses not to refuse to close the poem as a book. In *Convergences*, Lionel Kearns "cannot guarantee" another of the "numberless endings" in his "continuous sense of disorder and confusion" (n.p.).

Another aspect of the prosody that gets generated through "estrangement" is silence. Erasures and absences. In *Africa's Rhythm and African Sensibility,* John Chernoff discusses the matrix in African drumming.

> *The music is perhaps best considered as an arrangement of gaps where one may add a rhythm, rather than as a dense pattern of sound. In the conflict of the rhythms, it is space between the notes from which the dynamic tension comes, and it is the silence which constitutes the musical form as much as does the sound (quoted in Mackey 30).*

And in a short essay called "Silence" the American poet Rae Armantrout lists some of the methods for achieving "cessation."

> *Suppose a writer wants to make room in her work for silence, for the experience of cessation; how is this accomplished?*
>
> 1. *She may end a line in her poem abruptly, unexpectedly somehow short of resolution.*
> 2. *She may create extremely tenuous connections between parts of a poem.*
> 3. *She may deliberately create the effect of inconsequence.*
> 4. *She may make use of self-contradiction or retraction.*
> 5. *She may use obvious ellipsis. She may use anything which places the existent in perceptible relation to the nonexistent, the absent or outside (30).*

The push for the long poem and narrative's ever-present cultural status has led to the resuscitation of the prose poem and other cross genre experiments. Brossard, Marlatt, Szumigalski, and many other women have been exploring this (though Brossard prefers the term "text.") Ron Silliman, in two essays, "The New Sentence" and "New Prose New Prose Poem," describes the recent re-emergence of the prose poem in the San Francisco area.

There could be problems keeping such tools as cadence, silence, and cross genre writing sharp, however, as these techniques become accepted, expected, and stylized. Again, at the

Long-liners conference, Nichol observed:

> *to alter is native to some of us, the desire to create the alter native tongue. but maybe the clue is to alter natives to narrative. that's what steve keeps saying. steve mccaffery keeps saying, "the real crisis is with the readers." we can't assume we're speaking their native tongue (87).*

Simon Watney, while revealing the Romantic roots of making strange, has traced the use of "ostranenie" as a technique in photography:

> *[T]he entire theory of making strange can be seen to have been rooted in a fundamentally bourgeois abstraction of "thought" from the rest of material life, with a strongly idealist emphasis on the determining primacy of ideas.*
>
> *[I]n practice the devices of "ostranenie" tended to become reified, to become seen as intrinsically "correct," at which point they slid into mannerism. They became vulnerable both to that Modernist aestheticism which values the innovative purely in stylistic terms for its own sake, and also to the totalitarian elements within the Romantic tradition which would*

> *seek to iron out all human differences, in the name of Art, the Proletariat, Truth or whatever. Thus making strange ceased to respond to the demands of specific historical situations, and collapsed into stylization (56).*

But I don't think it is simply or only a matter of history or ideology. "Ostranenie" is a compositional stance. Writing needs to generate fresh perception, even after the strange becomes familiar.

Spun between Freud and Foucault, in *Psychic Life*, Judith Butler offers some interesting analysis on "Subjection, Resistance, Resignification" that would help reconfigure much of this stuff on estrangement in the context of attention to the subjected body.

Politics and the Referent

Steve McCaffery's notes on "language-centered, de-referential writing" in a 1977 issue of *Open Letter* focuses on what continues to be a fundamental concern to those of us who are interested in the language of poetry as a means of recovering or sustaining a value in life:

> *to centre language inside itself; to show the essential subjectless-ness a text might be; to stress the disemotional and dereferential possibilities of language as fragmentary, yet intensely*

> *direct experience. Language then, for itself, but for the sake of us. To step outside of use. To counter-communicate in order . . . to see what a hammer is when not in function ("Death" 61).*

McCaffery's indications oriented us to an underlying political writing stance in the US and in Canada. Nicole Brossard had for years undertaken a discourse intentionally sighted to intervene on "Mr." Language, the Catholic Church, the Canadian Confederation, and the literary establishment.

> *So all together those three realities set up for me a social and literary field that I could oppose and later on transgress and subvert. Very early my poetry was abstract, syntactically nonconventional; desire with its erotic drives had a great part in it. Part of what I was writing was consciously political, at least at the level of intention. Let's say that my "basic intention" was to make trouble, to be a troublemaker in regard to language but also with values of my own embodied by a writing practice that was ludic (playing with words), experimental (trying to understand processes of writing), and exploratory (searching). You see, it brings us*

back to my values: exploration (which provides for renewal of information and knowledge), intelligence (which provides the ability to process things), and pleasure (which provides for energy and desire) ("Poetic" 77).

Brossard is undoubtedly the most political writer in what used to be Canada (that is, the Canada prior to its being almost totally hijacked by the corporate right), and the forum for tactical intervention and the poetics of the potent she has voiced access to continues to cultivate possibility for not only a large and powerful feminist writing constituency but for writers seeking to sever perpetual sameness in any sense.

This is a debate, an argument, of course. Problems of meaning, aboutness, clarity, intellectualism. For some, now, a bit of a conundrum. A recent statement by a fairly normative and accessible lyric poet, Andrew Wreggitt, discusses the snag.

So there's a problem here. I refuse to write things that are incomprehensible and don't touch people on anything more than a 'isn't-that-clever' level. At the same time, there's no point in me writing the same book over and over. Invoking closure on myself. There's something else I want to get at in my poetry but I don't know exactly what it is or how I'm going to do it. There's just a feeling floating back there . . . So What am I gonna do? I dunno. I don't know (27).

Negative capability? The writer knowing how to not know.

A large part of this debate gets formally centered on new narrative techniques, parafictions, prose poems, and so forth; forms that Geoff Hancock aligns to "New Directions in Fiction and Physics." A more muffled kind of rhetoric hovers around what Doug Barbour incisively locates as "lyric/anti-lyric." And in a special issue of *Ellipse* on "New Love Poetry," Michel Beaulieu notices, already in 1980, "the strong comeback of the I, of lyricism, of the *readable,* of a vocabulary that some writers, despite the main trends that flourished in the past ten years, had never abandoned during that time" (11).

The politics of the referent, and of the "I," and certainly now in unbundling Canada's nineties, of "I"dentity, continues to buffer the text.

•◆•

The continuing friction between radical and mainstream on issues of formal innovation and social change, on a speaking and spoken "I," on experience versus representation, and so on, becomes even more complicated as it is inserted into an agenda of race, class, and global ideology.

•◆•

Trans=geo=ethno=poetics

By now in this consideration of the implements of estrangement, particularly with the subsuming power of the more apparent "politics of reputation by . . . those 'official' arbiters of taste, the anthologies and their editors" (Nichol, "In/Ov" 1), the toolbox lies dispersed in a scatter and a frenzy of needs. The more urgent poetics and politics associated with fictocriticism, the body, and the referent become sharp fragments of focus and activity. I've fabricated the term "trans=geo=ethno=poetics" as a convenient complex for what's left.

Some tilt towards translation, transcreation, seems always necessary within the Canadian poetic. *Open Letter* has documented much of the dialogue of the Toronto Research Group (bpNichol and Steve McCaffery) on modes of translation, one of which underlies bpNichol's progenerative series "Translating Translating Apollinaire." Colin Browne edited an issue of *Ellipse* (29/30, 1982) devoted to the serial translation of six poets. *Tessera* has focused on the bilinguality of Lola Lemire Tostevin's writing (6, Spring 1989). The translational/transcreative process behaves as a part of another term, the "potent," described by George Bowering as that which "resides in . . . the possible combinations and recombinations of the basic materials of . . . language" ("Power" 102) and noted earlier by Daphne Marlatt regarding her translation of a Tostevin poem.

> *in translating a poem that so intensively works the language it seems already a translation of that original struggle between intent and language drift, the translation (becomes) process embeds metatranslation while the*

> *target language not wanting to replace / consume the resonance of the source language oscillates in potential conversation with it ("Vers-ions" 19).*

Translation, then, transcreation; not distanced from the source but movement to the source.

Sometimes the source is the *geo,* place. In an expansive review of eleven books, Andy Suknaski seeks to locate his coordinates of a northern *imago mundi,* "[o]ut of Naryan to bifrost/the word arresting entropy" (5–6). In a philosophical meandering on Robert Kroetsch's *Field Notes,* Ed Dyck zeroes in on "recursion" as the power of place in poetry. "Place is a nest of words," he says. "When the poet builds his nest he creates place, he does not define it. The world, paradoxically, is laid in place, not the other way around. An immediate corollary, of course, is that the poet lays the egg" (23). Rudy Wiebe investigates the areal reality of the north in his recent book, *Playing Dead.* Aritha van Herk calls her book, *Places Far From Ellesmere,* a "geografictione."

And the *geo* isn't only a prairie concern. There's west and east. Bowering seeks to describe "the little shrinking strands of the west that are still left . . . usually called the last of something"("Western" 17–18). Gail Scott imagines the Québécois milieu: "For regardless of the language we speak, the culture we live in, we always have the double sense of both belonging and being excluded . . . Standing on the outside—the better, perhaps, to create" ("Virginia" 34).

Recent margins of the native and ethnic are also standing on the outside, creating, or trying to. People of colour, particularly women, are vocalizing their need for languages which are their own. The Caribbean English voice is strong with writers like Dionne Brand, Marlene Nourbese Philip, and Claire Harris. Asian-Canadian writers such as Jim Wong-Chu, Sky Lee, Roy Miki, Gerry Shikatani, and myself, seek to redress and rewrite the colonizing racism of western transnational ideologies.

When Elijah Harper beached Meech, the agitated pertinence of such Aboriginal voices as Lee Maracle, Jeannette Armstrong, Daniel David Moses, and Lenore Keeshig Tobias hummed with baited breath and new words on the periphery. Listen to this chunk of krinopoeia by Marie Annharte Baker from "Raced Out to Write this Up":

> *I often race to write I write about race why do I*
> *write about race I must erase all trace of my*
> *race I am an eraser abrasive bracing myself*
> *embracing*
>
> *it is classic to want to write about class not low*
> *class but up the nose class I know I am classy*
> *brassy crass ass of a clash comes when I move*
> *up a rung*
>
> *we are different skins different bins for brown*

rice and white rice not even a container of wild
rice you know what they do when you are
white and not rich poverty counts big when
you count the cost of a caste a colourful past

•◆•

Through the nineties I've adjusted some of the above poetics to address issues of formal innovation and racialization in writing. During my writing life the possibilities of thinking in poetry have shifted, though not as radically as we might think. Political and social frames have surfaced that enable a broad range of poetic singularities, particularly for marginalized writers (and their histories).

•◆•

Strangle Two

> *If the surface of the page is really synchronous with activity then the true morphology of alterity, "the cedar-head that needs the cedar-feet," the round and the square, the feathers the iron the crack the stone, names still occupied by thought territory, syntax of the re-, routing and writing, all in order to make poetry movement visible, to right "the lightning flash that connects heaven and earth" off of its habitual lodestone, not just flip the magnets "four steps; negative/positive (forward) & negative/positive (backward), or no-yes/no-yes" but still some emic vessel that narrates the dialogue home, water, egg.*

That braille-like surfacing of juncture with all the material you can get hold of. The potent. Otherness as alteration, altered (not altared). Olson's dirt still dangling from the roots. Not so much to get out of the egg but to get it back. Talking to yourself, you, talking back, and forth. I mean "home" as a verb: Sammy the Salmon.

In the Summer '93 issue of *Books in Canada*, the editor of *Exile* magazine, Barry Callaghan, puzzles

> *that the children of immigrants, and the children of the children of immigrants, still do not seem to be writing about Canadian experience in a Canadian language. God, this is what W. W. E. Ross, our first modern poet, pleaded for in the 1920s. So what do we find? As I look in this teeming city for more and more evidence of language and place, I am confronted with an enthusiasm, an official enthusiasm, for writers who have settled here from abroad, and write out of that foreign experience (13).*

"Please understand me," he whines on, "I am not complaining about the authenticity of their voice, it's real and good, but it isn't the language of here. It's more levitation" (13).

Another powerplay pitch from what considers itself to be centre-field (eastern Canada) and centre-fold, Callaghan wants to define authentic Canadian literature as writing bound and gagged to the imaginary called Canada. Rohinton Mistry, Michael Ondaatje, Claire Harris, Sam Selvon, if they really want to live here, had better not write about Bombay, North Africa, or the Caribbean. Callaghan reckons Austin Clarke's okay because he's "capturing the rhythms of Black people in our city streets" (13). What a fresh insight: Black people and rhythm.

Callaghan's sense of place and poetry is a proprietary construction of a geo-political aesthetic. Canada has happily been shaped for him as the apple of John A. MacDonald's eye, fishless sea to fishless sea. He's worried that some foreign *imago mundi* is contaminating our measure of where we live and (same thing) our measure of CanLit. Our. Us. Us—them. W. W. E. Ross is certainly not my first modern poet. I've seen Callaghan's and MacDonald's and Ross's Canada as it has tried and keeps trying to put me in their place. Witness Brian Mulroney's attempt at the NAFTA symposium, June 1999: "There are times when Canadians must be told not what they want to know but what they need to know."

Their Canada isn't. For me. Not the same anything when you're half Swede, quarter Chinese, and quarter Ontario Wasp. My hybridity obliges me to locate by difference, not sameness. My sense of place has become informed by distinctive features, particulars, sometimes minute particulars. In fact, the landscape of this large and hypothetical country seems to me best known and valorized by the singular. And the plurality that gets generated thus is less troublesome than the exclusive kind of singularity implied by Callaghan's "we." Place therefore seems specific and particular. Where one is, here, is who one is, albeit contaminated at times by the sledgehammer tactics of the Wasp hive.

Detained on this island
at the gates of Gold Mountain
brings to my throat a hundred feelings.

So laments a Chinese immigrant writing on the walls of his detention jail cell in Victoria. (Someone else's first modern poet?) What Callaghan's sensibility does not acknowledge, of course, is that the "here" comes with full banks of memory, part of an *anima mundi*, a spirit that no cultural nationalism can subvert.

But the friction of difference seems necessary fuel, crucial to a poetics of ethnicity in this country, a poetics of the potent. As Myrna Kostash has pointed out, "We may wish to remind ourselves, over and over, that we live on the wrong side of the tracks, on the edge of town" (19).

That's it, the local. What is meant in the west by the term regional. The immediate "here," the palpable, tangible "here," imprinted with whatever trailing cellular memory, histology, history, story. These are not "our city streets," these are my city streets, and you better not be out to "capture" anything, the rhythms of Black people, or anybody's rhythm. As Dionne Brand says, "Maybe [you] didn't notice but [your] hand is in my pocket" ("Who" 15).

The shape of a dissonant conjunction in writing comes from the energy of otherness created by the movement to reclaim the self from the tendency to privilege the apparent from the hidden, the morpheme from the eme.

> *Put yourself inside the head of a bird as he's flying down a channel of water. Okay. Now the*

> *image would be what you see if you're outside on the bank looking up at him. That's not what I'm interested in. I'm interested in getting you inside his head in flight. And everything's moving. There is no still reference point because he's in flight, you're in flight. Whoever's reading* (Marlatt, "Given" 79).

The shape is filled with necessity, and with all the anxiety of either being recognized (recognizable) or not. Nellie Wong, for example, garbs her lyric form not only to document but also to see through a scenario of identity:

> *At the edge of the plaza*
> *a young girl leans against a gray wall.*
> *She is a donut, half raised.*
> *The men who watch her*
> *finger themselves/ inside their pockets.*
>
> *I tell myself:*
> *I am not she, I am not she.*
> *She is someone else's sister* (38).

How to pick up one end of the stick and not the other?

John Thorpe's prologue to John Clarke's *From Feathers to Iron* cites a short story by W. B. Yeats in which two men are talking and, at one point, one turns to the other and says: "You know, we're very unlike each other: you're all feathers on one end of the shaft, and I'm all iron on the tip." And Clarke says, "Don't take from systems which don't have to do with your experience of otherness . . . Otherwise, it can become an occasion for speculation or, worse, fundamentalist belief" (xv).

We can only half get this, this option of the particular, the singular. The temptation (interpellation) just to be the "shaft" is strong.

> *Why would this Portuguese sailor come over to*
> *me and in his broken English point to the tatoo*
> *[sic] of a geisha as if I would identify with it.*
> *And I did a little (Hahn, n.p.).*

Shape as a verb. That's one way to intercept the virtual or imaginary proxies of experience (e.g., home is how, not where, you hang your hat) as they subsume their positions of authority and control. To modulate is to act.

The wedges and chisels used to split stone are likewise called feathers and irons. Stonescape.

A Poetics of Ethnicity

Stances towards writing that have arisen out of an ethnic response demonstrate inventions of alignment and resistance. Immigrant, ethnic, and native writers in Canada have utilized most of the available public aesthetics in order to create a more satisfying space within which to investigate their particular realities. For some writers this entails an alignment with mainstream and traditional strategies while for others the tactics of refusal and reterritorialization offer a more appropriate poetics.

I use the term "poetics" here not in the theoretical sense of the study of or theory about literature, but in its practical and applied sense, as the tools designed or located by writers and artists to initiate movement and change. That is, "poetics as a sort of *applied poetic*, in the sense that engineering is a form of applied mathematics"(Bernstein, "Optimism" 151). The culturally marginalized writer will engineer approaches to language and form that enable a particular residue (genetic, cultural, biographical) to become kinetic and valorized. For Canadian writers like Joy Kogawa and Rohinton Mistry, the stance is to operate within a colonized and inherited formal awareness while investigating their respective enactments of internment and migration. But others, such as Roy Kiyooka and Marlene Nourbese Philip, operating from spatial allocations similar to those of Kogawa and Mistry, have chosen to utilize more formal innovative possibilities. This second group of writers seems to me to embody an approach that might properly be called something like "alienethnic" poetics. This poetics, while often used for its ethnic imprint and frequently originating from the necessity to complicate difference, is certainly not limited to an ethnic "project"; the same tactics could as well be used for other goals. Feminist poetics, for example, have arguably contributed some of the most useful means to compose ethnic intention.

Margaret Atwood's notion that "[w]e are all immigrants to this place even if we were born here" (62), quoted by Rosemary Sullivan in "Who are the immigrant writers and what have they done," seems only to universalize the "many" as "one." A "poetics of ethnicity" would be, then, in the view of Atwood and Sullivan, simply *the* poetics, the whole *Canadian* thing. But a practical and applied "poetics" is a singular and personal toolbox and a writer who seeks to articulate a distinctive ethnic and, as I shall suggest, ethical sensibility requires particular and circumstantial poetics, the right tools.

For example, in his essay "The Ethnic Voice in Canadian Writing," Eli Mandel rebounds from Atwood's claim to point to a particular "ethnic strategy":

> *It is not only that as strangers we find ourselves in a strange land, but with the burden upon us as well . . . of living simultaneously . . . in doubleness, that is difficult enough. To articulate*

> *that doubleness simply intensifies the pressure, the burden. But there is a further step in which what Atwood calls "inescapable doubleness" turns into duplicity, a strategy for cultural identification that I take to be the ethnic strategy, the 'voice' I'm trying to identify (264–265).*

The duplicitous voice, then, is what's needed and gets placed in the ethnopoetic toolbox. As indicated by Mandel (266), Robert Kroetsch subsumes the identity question into fiction's role, and Linda Hutcheon, in her introduction to *Other Solitudes: Canadian Multicultural Fictions*, cites Aritha van Herk as claiming fiction as a "refuge" from multicultural or ethnic "displacement" (5). Fiction's double-dealing hand is seen as the result of a move from the familiar to the foreign.

In an article on "Dialogism and the Canadian Novel" Sherrill Grace lists some of the chicanery available in the novelist trickster's bag of double-voicing and polyphony: refraction of words, voices, and characters; parody; polemically coloured autobiography and confession; hybrid languages; carnivalization; inserted genres such as diaries, letters, found documents; Kroetsch's syncretic "provocation of the word by the word" (121). She adds:

> *At first glance, it would seem that politically, geographically, and linguistically Canada, unlike the United States, constitutes the perfect dialogistic space. To paraphrase Bakhtin in* The

> Dialogic Imagination, *we believe that we lack a truly unifying mythology; we behave as if politically decentered, and we try to allow for (or actualize) ethnic and linguistic diversity. As a result, "verbal-ideological decentring" should occur here because, as a "national culture," we have never had a "sealed-off and self-sufficient character" and have always thought of ourselves as "only one among other cultures and languages" (131–132).*

Why then, asks the non-aligned writer, the fighter, does the monologic tradition dominate in fiction? What is this longing for unity? This desire for centres?

I've noticed, in the jockeying for the position of voice debate, that the term "ethnic" has been shunned as "incorrect" or "unusable" as a description of nonmainstream, visible/invisible minority, marginalized, race, origin, native, or otherwise "Other." Linda Hutcheon, for example, argues for the use of the term "multicultural" as a more inclusive term instead of "ethnic" which "always has to do with the social positioning of the 'other', and is thus never free of relations of power and value" (2). To me, her rationale is similar to Atwood's view of a generic immigrant experience. Hutcheon admits that the issues associated with the term "ethnic" are, in fact, "the very issues raised by the structure of [their] book, as well as by the individual voices within it" (2). Though Hutcheon claims to want to challenge "the hierarchy of social and cultural privilege" (2), her apparent contradiction threatens to nullify the move.

This Greek-Indo-European term has provided a useful poetic accommodation. The etymon *eth* surfaced for me years ago when I struggled with the notions of "earth" and "ethos." Here is the poem that revealed to me a set of lasting keywords.

> *Eth means why any one returns*
> *every one all over the place they are in*
> *entwined into the confluence of the two rivers*
> *into the edges of a genetic inscription*
> *and our homes and loves now night*
> *spreads out up the valleys*
> *into the many-forgotten messages and arrangements*
> *carried there the character sticks*
> *hunger* (Earth *n.p.)*

So the tools of place, genetic inscription, home, love, message, and hunger have clung like dirt to those roots.

I should mention that I now understand these tools to be somewhat faulty and suspect as they become ultimately implicated as consumable imaginaries in global exchange.

Useful in alienethnic poetics is, of course, the Deleuze/Guattari term of reterritorialization seen by Barbara

Godard in Lola Lemire Tostevin's "The place becomes writing . . . " and Smaro Kamboureli's gloss on Tostevin's language as "the graph of place" (Godard 160), and Kamboureli's own writing as "dealing with the self as 'the place of language'" (Williamson 34). The "nomadology" (Deleuze and Guattari) of the ethnic writer, that is the figuring out where she is, where to go, how to move, not just through language but in the world, is an investigation of place, as well as of placement in said place. For some, this is a reclamation project—and who could blame them, the natives. Jeannette Armstrong calls it the "Blood of My People."

forward   a red liquid   stream   that draws
ground upward   that shakes   earth and dust   to move
to move   a long line   before settling
quietly   back   into   soil (Telling It 57)

Because Armstrong's writing within English and not the native familiarity of her own Okanagan Salish, the gaps that punctuate her poem reflect the nomadic cut and refuse to settle into English's placement of expected syntax and, more basically and politically, into both the imaginary nation and its ideological assault on the land.

Furthermore, place is home or cave (including cave of self). But that ethos-ethnos leads to "ethic," *right* way. As I came to it in a prose poem where a lot of my old keywords tumbled forward.

MUSIC AT THE HEART OF THINKING NINETY

On the weekend I got into anger talk about landscape and the hunger of narrative to eat answer or time but space works for me because place got to be more spiritual at least last felt now this watery genetic I suspect passions like anger suprafixed to simply dwells I mean contained as we speak of it believe me I'd like to find a new word-track for feeling but language and moment work out simply as simultaneous occurrences so I don't think you should blame words for time-lapse tropism eg ethics is probably something that surrounds you like your house it's where you live.

Ethnic, ethic. A kind of anagogical exegesis of text that is a poetics of reading writing, and is particularly attractive to the ethnic sensibility because of its nomadic movement, as well as that world-sense of Truth-slash-El Dorado Quest for, and including traditional notions of, value, Idealism, Positivism, Moralism and even the present political/religious and economic globalism. What I'm trying to indicate is that the truth-track for the poetics of ethnicity vis-à-vis its sister dangling root, ethic, i.e., "where you live," is also "Other," a larger poetics term particularly attractive to contemporary ethnopoetics. Octavio Paz writes:

> *As to the discovery, I shall begin by saying that the concrete life is the real life, as against the uniform living that contemporary society tries to impose on us. [André] Breton has said:* la véritable existence est ailleurs. *That elsewhere is here, always here and in this moment. Real life opposes neither the quotidian nor the heroic life; it is the perception of the spark of the* otherness ... *(Clarke 151).*

To write (or live) ethnically is also to write (or live) ethically, in pursuit of right value, right place, right home, right otherness. The editors of *Shakti's Words*, an anthology of South Asian Canadian women's poetry, claim that Himani Bannerji's "ethic of individual responsibility, counterpointed by her recognition of external forces which imprison, is the coherent element in poems treating such topics as the cultural construction of woman and wife . . . and the immigrant's vibrant connection to her homeland" (McGifford xi). The poem they're referring to is a powerful indictment of apartheid that Bannerji puns as "Apart-Hate."

Michael Thorpe, in an assault on Arun Mukherjee's *Towards an Aesthetics of Opposition,* is bothered by a poetics of the "other." He asks, "Why would anyone not driven by material necessity . . . emigrate to and remain in an alien country and society in which they feel condemned to adopt a posture of opposition?" (4). Thorpe, and many others who are attracted to notions of alignment and "shared common values" (1), might well feel disturbed by a poetics of difference. For the writer addressing an ethnicity directed at other values, the naming and reterritorialization are fundamental to creative action, and so any move to articulate a re-found territory requires this other-side-of-the-tracks stance.

This is always threatening to the "other" other-side-of-the-tracks because, at least here in Canada, it is politically and ideologically tied to the redress and rewrite of the apple of John A. MacDonald's eye—the current debate on national unity. The moral reading of place-poetics argues, as Myrna Kostash does, for a named and functional tool of "otherness":

> *I had the very odd experience of finding myself entered in the* Oxford Companion to Canadian Literature *as "Kostash, Myrna, See; Ukrainian Writing." Odd, because it seems to me that, over some twenty years of writing, I have made a contribution not just as an ethnic but as a woman/feminist, an Albertan, a Canadian, a nonfictionist, organization activist, teacher—why should the "Ukrainian" component of all this activity be the one to characterize me? Odd, too, in that I have no idea what "Ukrainian writing" is supposed to mean in my case; I write only in English and address an English-speaking audience. What on earth does it take to become a Canadian writer, a contributor to and practi-*

> *tioner of CanLit, if not books written in Canada by a Canadian for Canadians? Could it be that, given my origins outside the Anglo-Celtic and Franco founding nations, I shall never be considered to belong because I wasn't there at the beginning when the naming took place? That CanLit is a category and a practice hijacked and held captive by a very exclusive gang of men and women who all come from the right side of the tracks? (18–19).*

She then goes on to negotiate for the position of the potent as she rejects the attempts at assimilation from the multicultural right side of the tracks. The exclusion, she points out,

> *is painful and exciting, for it is in those "interstices" of cultures that we have become writers. In other words, we may not* wish *to belong to the club. We may wish to live with tension and distress. We may wish to remind ourselves, over and over, that we live on the wrong side of the tracks, on the edge of town (19).*

Kostash is indicating the position of applied, chosen, desired, and necessary estrangement that has become a primary unit of composition for many Canadian writers as they seek to deterritorialize inherited literary forms and language, as they seek a heat through friction. This is a poetics of paradox. We know ourselves by our resistances, a teacher once instructed me.

Milagros Paredes:

> *And I move . . . not forward, but in all the directions my questions take me. I move tentatively, having always to remind myself that surrendering to my confusion will lead me to some kind of clarity (*Fireweed *77).*

This principle of synchronous foreignicity, akin to biology's Gaiic catastrophism, of embracing antithesis, polarity, confusion, and opposition as the day-to-day household harmony, is a necessary implement in art that looks for new organizing principles, new narratives.

Jam Ismail:

> *Read this book from right to left, reader dear (n.p.).*

Himani Bannerji:

> *A whole new story has to be told, with fragments, with disruptions, and with self-conscious and critical reflections. And one has to do it right . . .* [there's that "ethic" at work] *. . . Creating seamless narratives, engaging in exercises in dramatic plot creating, simply make cultural brokers, propagators of orientalism and self-reificationists out of us. My attempt here*

has been to develop a form which is both fragmentary and coherent in that it is both creative and critical—its self-reflexivity breaking through self-reification, moving towards a fragmented whole (Fireweed 134; *emphasis added).*

Edward Said:

A part of something is for the foreseeable future going to be better than all of it. Fragments over wholes. Restless nomadic activity over the settlements of held territory. Criticism over resignation. The Palestinian as self-consciousness in a barren plain of investments and consumer appetites. The heroism of anger over the begging bowl . . . To do as others do, but somehow to stand apart. To tell your story in pieces, as it is (150).

Anger. You can feel a bit of it, too, in Himani Bannerji's statement. And that "anger" in my own prose poem above ("On the weekend I got into anger") is the response of presence to the genetic other, a posed biotext in response to some ancestral ghosts. But I'm not alone. Here's Di Brandt:

I have tried everything, obedience, disobedience, running away, coming back, forgetting (blanking it out), recalling it again out of the dark,

> *killing it off, translating, leaving it. . . . sometimes i feel like screaming for them, sometimes i feel like screaming at them. sometimes i long to go back to my grandmother's garden . . . i hate having to choose between my inherited identity & my life: traditional Mennonite versus contemporary Canadian woman writer, yet how can i be both & not fly apart?* (Prairie Fire 183).

Such conflict gets knotted into the *ethos*, the right place, the "community."

This is Wednesday morning in Calgary, February 27, 1991. External Affairs Minister Joe Clark phones me and invites me to participate in a discussion he's holding with some other artists on Saturday night in Calgary. The topic is national unity. What he wants is our "imagination," our Image Nation. He says he's concerned about the body of much of the discussion on national unity drifting too heavily towards "laws" and "legislation" and such "business." While he talks to me I keep thinking, "Why isn't he somewhere else doing something about peace in the mid-east? Why isn't he busy deconstructing Canada's surreptitious arms economy?" And just before he phoned, as I said, I was reading Himani Bannerji's poem "Apart-hate":

> *In this white land*
> *Where I wander with scape-goats*

there are laws

Apart-hate

. . .

. . .

In this white land

skin is fingered like pelt

skin is sold and the ivory of her eyes

the category human has no meaning

when spoken in white

Apart-hate (13–14)

You can imagine the resin in my own imagination at the time. I told Mr. Clark that, unfortunately, I'd be at a conference on multiculturalism in Winnipeg that evening. Don't get me wrong. I appreciate being asked. I wish, in some ways, I could be there, mouthing my own disjointed diatribe against the centre. I wonder if I would be able to talk about the non-aligned poetics of ethnicity,

or Kostash's deep need for opposition,

and Uma Parameswaran's "questions" (66)
at the end of every word,

or Di Brandt's anger,

and Roy Kiyooka's
unwelcome but salutary silences . . . [and] tied
tongue. ("We Asian" n.p.)

or Gerry Shikatani's

the sign
mouth becomes

to throw
all weapons
into the cave of words (*frontispiece*)

and Kristjana Gunnars' *Carnival of Longing*

or Roy Miki's "fear . . . in the face of racism" (*Saving Face* xi),
his "museum of mirrors
on the far side of town" (*Saving Face* 14)

and Marie Annharte Baker's racing
to write I write about race why do I write about race
I must erase all trace of my race I am an eraser
abrasive bracing myself embracing (1)

or Marlene Nourbese Philip's question,
if no one sings the note between the silences
. . .
is it still music (117)

and the community in Sky Lee's *Disappearing Moon Cafe*

or Claire Harris' "Grammar of the Heart"
How here to say the unsayable (54)

and Jim Wong-Chu's

lost . . .

on earth

above the bones

of a multitude

of golden mountain men (21)

or Lee Maracle's trickster Raven,
another trick tucked within her wings (30)

and Daphne Marlatt's

> you, caught out in a language that sounded strange,
> stranger yourself, deprived of words that spoke what
> you knew ("In the Month" 94)

or David Arnason's "writing as carpentry" (9)

and Phyllis Webb's "Leaning"

> slumped one degree from the horizontal
>
> the whole culture leaning . . .
>
> . . .
>
> And you, are you still here
>
> tilted in this stranded ark
> blind and seeing in the dark (*Water and Light* 58–59).

or Nicole Brossard's

> intention . . . to make trouble. to be a troublemaker
> in regard to language but also with values of my
> own ("Poetic" 77).

Well there's the rub, Joe. The tactical imagination of a "national unity" is, for some writers, a "disunity." And the ethnopoetics tool box isn't even only "ethnic," at least in the sense of racial. These tools are shared by writers who are marginalized, invisible, experimental, political, and in need of any tool that might imagine a culture that could recognize an alien identity and construct a common language of the other.

Strangle Three

> *Some critical digit stutter of knowing both entrance and exit and that same trestle same deep gully of poem tunnel coming through strapped to mind dubbed image a hail of intonation that moment's Chinese river nation zero still packed with caboodle these signals putting in fatal time pause fast forward rewind.*

The exploration of identity that locates the self so that the outside's coming in; some device that trips the signal of a vortex of self-knowledge not excluding all that out there (like nation) but simply reversing the force into self-motion, a kind of domestication of the ambient. When she called me a Chink I could see the kit that came with the call. Later the turbulence, not of the name but outside the name. All wrapped up and nowhere to go but under.

Inside the devices of knowing are the projects of completion. What prevents their mediocrity is to materialize the form through some kind of movement, react to it, and then put it inside/outside/alongside another form.

One two three four five six five four three two one is how *How Two* by Kathryn MacLeod invites this narrative, almost lyric, "you" to gesture lightly to form so that something like "Jack, I will not allow you to extend a) an arm / b) an invitation" really gets operating room in a mind that looks for another story. That is, the implicit authority of the "I" is temporary and writing looks for a minding way out, an ethics of subjectivity, an opening that releases the person from language's requirements for authority.

Diaspora could be like that (instead of nostalgic authentication). Self needs to be distracted from the complete sentence, kept poetent. *Jamelie•Jamila Project, a collaborative bookwork* by j. hassan & j. ismail is designed as a folder filled with poems, stories, plays, drawings, paintings, photos, and documents. The folder, with interior pockets, is panelled on both sides: the inside shows photos from the Gaza occupation (you have to look under the flaps to see some of the soldiers) and handwriting ("The woman one cannot, geopolitically, imagine enough to love/be loved, singly in gift") over graffiti; the outside jacket has a title in Arabic, *dur-a-sat*, the root of the word "to study." jamelie hassan told me that this means "studying ourselves, our genealogy, our names." The jacket also includes the text of a screenplay, "Casa Blanca," by j.i.

The items in the folder are six separate sheets of various texts and documents, a "Season Greetings" card from The Association of Artists—Gaza Strip, a small "77" notebook from China, a tea-card-poem (with a bag of Yunnan tea), and a twenty-page chapbook of poems, statements, and photos.

The fragmentation is a useful way to display the parallel energies of these two artists. Though only the design of the bookwork is collaborative, we see a contiguous bordering of comparable contents: immigration, identity, conflict, naming, Palestine, Hong Kong, Canada. The power of the presentation is in how the particular attentions of these two artists run side-by-side. j.i.'s expansive and incisive care to ground each word and phrase in her poems corresponds to j.h.'s relentless focus on the tangible in power politics. For example, in one two-page spread in the chapbook, we have a selection from j.i.'s "scared texts" that highlight her mindfulness of race and class juxtaposed with a colour reproduction of j.h.'s painting of newspaper, tomatoes, irises, and ginger root entitled *Trial of the Gang of Four, 1981*. One of the poems is j.i.'s interrogative swirl of identities:

> ratio quality   *young ban yen*
> *had been thought italian in*
> *kathmandu, filipina in hong kong,*
> *eurasian in kyoto, japanese in*
> *anchorage, dismal in london england,*
> *hindu in edmonton,*
> *generic oriental in calgary, western*
> *canadian in ottawa, anglo-phone in*
> *montreal, métis in jasper, eskimo at*
> *hudson's bay department store,*
> *vietnamese in chinatown, tibetan in*
> *vancouver, commie at the u.s.*
> *border.*
>
> *on the whole very asian.*

Then, a little further on, is a text and image by j.h. about a Chinese cafe in London.

Notions of race and class conflict are interlaced with the two women's intentions of ferreting out identity and name, Jamelie—Jamila. The play and suggestiveness are at the surface—tangling, probing. One of the great advantages to this kind of bookwork is how much these artists leave open; the potency of process is left intact: the questions can keep coming. And do.

Beyond the kit I could see the caboodle.

Half-Bred Poetics

UNTIL MARY MCNUTTER CALLS ME A CHINK I'M not one. That's in elementary school. Later, I don't have to be because I don't look like one. But just then, I'm stunned. I've never thought about it. After that I start to listen, and watch. Some people are different. You can see it. Or hear it.

The old Chinamen have always been friends of my dad's. They give us kids candy. I go fishing down by the boathouses with one of them. He's a nice man, shiny brown knuckles, baits my hook, shows me how to catch mud-suckers, shows me how to row a boat. We're walking back up the hill with our catch of suckers and some kids start chinky, chinky Chinaman and I figure I'd better not be caught with him anymore.

I become as white as I can, which, considering I'm mostly Scandinavian, is pretty easy for me. Not for my dad and some of my cousins though. They're stuck, I think, with how they look. I only have the name to contend with. And I not only hear my friends put down the Chinks (and the Japs, and the Wops, and the Spiks, and the Douks) but comic books and movies confirm that the Chinese are yellow (meaning cowardly), not to be trusted, heathens, devils, slant-eyed, dirty, and talk incomprehensible gobblydee-gook. Thus, gook n. Slang. 1. A dirty, sludgy, or slimy substance. 2. An Oriental. An offensive term used derogatorily. Even now a half-Ukrainian-half-Japanese daughter of a friend of mine calls anyone, white or not, who doesn't fit, a Geek. Even her father, who, we all know, is really a Nip.

Sticks and stones might break my bones, but names will never hurt me (Diamond *98).*

That's from a prose biotext I've written called *Diamond Grill.* It's a text that interrogates the roots of my own anger as racial—genetically and culturally. It's only one of a number of diatribes against the assumptions and confusions of identity I feel compelled to reconfigure, as the recent bag of re- poetics (recuperate, rewrite, transport, transform, and so forth) proffers. The site of this poetics for me, and many other multiracial and multi-cultural writers, is the hyphen, that marked (or unmarked) space that both binds and divides. This henopoetic (Grk heno-, one) punct, this flag of the many in the one, yet "less than one and double" (Bhabha 177), is the operable tool that both compounds difference and underlines sameness.

Though the hyphen is in the middle, it is not in the centre. It is a property marker, a boundary post, a borderland, a bastard, a railroad, a last spike, a stain, a cypher, a rope, a knot, a chain (link), a foreign word, a warning sign, a head tax, a bridge, a no-man's land, a nomadic, floating magic carpet, now you see it now you don't. The hyphen is the hybrid's dish, the mestiza's whole wheat tortillas (Anzaldua 194), the Metis' apple (red on the outside, white on the inside), the happa's egg (white out, yellow in), the mulatto's café au lait.

I want to focus here on the scene of the *hyphen* as a crucial location for working at hybridity's implicit ambivalence. In order to actualize this hybridity, what Bhabha sees as "a negative transparency that comes to be agonistically constructed *on the boundary* between frame of reference/frame of mind" (175), the hybrid writer must (one might suspect, necessarily) develop instruments of disturbance, dislocation, and displacement. The hyphen, even when it is notated, is often silent and transparent. I'd like to make the noise surrounding it more audible, the pigment of its skin more visible. But, and this is essential to the use of the hyphen as a tool, "It is not a question of harmonizing with the background," as Lacan writes, "but, against a mottled background, of being mottled—exactly like the technique of camouflage practiced in human warfare" (cited in Bhabha 181). This is, after all, as Claire Harris reminds us, "dangerous territory":

but they go three women
into the uncharted self they go
looking out for each other
and following the blood
as one follows a river
through dangerous

territory
in darkness
camouflaged (10)

Bhabha has described hybridity as a persistent thorn in the side of colonial configurations, rather than "a third term that resolves the tension between two cultures" (175). This constant pressure that the hyphen brings to bear against the master narratives of duality, multiculturalism, and apartheid creates a volatile space that is inhabited by a wide range of voices. My own interest in the site and sign of the hyphen is essentially from a blood quantum point of view, that is, as a "mixed blood." Others occupy the site as immigrants, or as visible minorities, or as political allies. Whoever they are, as writers, they have a poetics available that helps materialize what has been otherwise "denied knowledges" (Bhabha 175). A hybrid borderland poetics.

The Writers' Union of Canada's Racial Minority Writers' Committee organized a conference for "writers of colour and first nations writers" and the workshop portion of the conference was only open to those who are "Writing Thru Race" (that is, it excluded whites). The event (Vancouver, June 30–July 3, 1994) caused quite a stir in the ongoing Canadian debate about the country's policy of multiculturalism. It's the usual confrontation with the liberal dogmatists of pluralism insisting on their unique devotion to generosity and tolerance (Mitchell 500) without reflection on how their philosophy operates as a strategy for the appropriation of power, or on how their anxiety reflects their melancholy over potential loss (of property, of gaze, of narrative) (Chow 1–5). The writers of colour and First Nations writers wanted, simply, to reserve a space of their own, for a total of seven and a half hours one weekend, free from the ongoing necessity to educate, report to, and soothe the dominant culture. They wanted not a separation, but a chance for a cross-cultural exchange where "cross-cultural" isn't only a white-crossed-with-everything else exchange. More and more, as race continues to rewrite its history, the "tentative coalitions being forged between the various so-called minority cultural communities are not only providing a respite from the confrontational aspect of white/other relationships, but are providing tremendous emotional support and a broader, kinder buffer zone within which to ally and act" (Lippard 196–197).

In opposition to a nationalistic aesthetic that continually attempts to expropriate difference into its own consuming narrative, writers of colour and Aboriginal writers gain a significant social empowerment by engaging in dialogues that relocate the responsibility for their own subjectivity within themselves. Even though many of these writers share in the avant-gardist tactics of borderland poetics and feminist poetics, they feel a strong need to participate in a tangible community (despite the cries of "separatist") in order to locate the cortex of their own social content without it being conditioned by first-world perceptions. Jeff Derksen's "Making Race Opaque" situates my own writing in this context as well as delineates the aesthetics of first-world expectation, a term he gets from Laura Kipnis' "Aesthetics and Foreign Policy."

Though those opposed to the "Writing Thru Race" conference claimed that everyone is hyphenated somehow (not unlike Margaret Atwood's insistence that all Canadians are immigrants anyway), my own hyphenation strikes a particular ambivalence. I can pass for white until I have to explain my name. And even though the blood quantum shows only one quarter Chinese, that name, Wah, is enough of a shade to mottle an otherwise apparent European background.

> (Vancouver, British Columbia 1963)
> *Hello, is this the US consulate? I'm calling about getting a visa. I'm going to Albuquerque as a graduate student but I'd like to be able to work in the States.*

What's your name?

Wah. Double U, Ay, Aych. Fred Wah.

Is that a Chinese name?

Yes it is. Why?

I'm afraid you'll have to apply under the Asian quota, sir, and there's a backup of several years on the Asian list.

But I'm a Canadian.

I'm afraid that doesn't matter. If you're of Chinese origin, even if you're born in Canada, you still have to go under the Asian quota.

Well that's ridiculous. Could I come down and talk to the Consul General about this?

By all means, but he's a busy . . .

I'll be right down.

(fast over False Creek down Burrard to Georgia —downtown)

And what can I do for you, sir?

My name's Fred Wah. I talked with the receptionist on the phone this morning about getting a visa. She told me that, even though I'm Canadian, because my racial origin is Chinese, I'll have to apply under the Asian quota.

But you don't look Chinese.

That's because I'm half-Swedish. I'm only quarter-Chinese.

Well, that makes all the difference then. If you're less than fifty per cent you can enter the US as a Canadian. Just ask the girl out front for the forms, it shouldn't take more than a few days.

You had me fooled there.[1]

I look through *The Big Aiiieeeee!: An Anthology of Chinese American and Japanese American Literature,* for Eurasians, checking out the balance and looking for new voices. I skip around and then realize I'm looking for clues in the names. Lawson Fusao Inada. "Lawson" suggests a trace of whiteness. Good poetry. Jazzy. Nice sense of line and rhythm. I go to his poem "On Being Asian American" (619) and notice he doesn't use a hyphen between Asian and American. I wonder if he thinks, as many racially/nationally-hyphenated people do, that the hyphen anchors and contains identity into a colonially constructed box. I look at other names. Wing Tek Lum—no. David Wong Louie—maybe. Jeffrey, Frank, John, Larry—what sort of hint am I looking for? Mixed names, like Fred Wah. But not mixed. Yet mixed.

I stop at Violet Kazue Matsuda de Cristoforo as a likely possibility. But no, several marriages have gauzed over her identity.

---

1 This piece was mistakenly left out of *Diamond Grill.*

And then there's Sui Sin Far, the chosen pseudonym for Edith Maud Eaton, a turn-of-the-century Eurasian American writer.

An article by another young Canadian writer, Kyo Maclear, reminds me of the writing of Han Suyin.

I email a writer friend in Vancouver, Scott Toguri McFarlane, a tall, white-skinned (like me) Eurasian. His Japanese roots are so hidden you can't see them and, when he doesn't foreground Toguri, you can't read them even in his name. I could have been like Scott if my father had been Swedish and my mother Chinese. Race concealed by the patronym of marriage.

So names and naming not only encounter a blood residue but also indicate the camouflage possibilities of the name (both visible and invisible, both dash and cypher). I need to look beyond obvious possibilities in names like John Yau and Mei Mei Berssenbrugge to locate the voices of Metis writer Maria Campbell and Okanagan writer Jeannette Armstrong. It is, after all, necessary to determine who occupies this hyphen, if not only to hear their different stories, then at least to read their texts for particular political and compositional possibilities.

We cannot take the names for granted since, when they have been manipulated and recycled by the language of the master, "we may not only read between the lines but even seek to change the often coercive reality that they so lucidly contain" (Bhabha 181). If we are mestiza, for example, we may need to engage the recuperative possibilities available through naming. In a fascinating account, Mary Louise Pratt tells how the name of La Malinche, the fourteen-year-old Aztec concubine of Hernán Cortés who helped the Spanish conquer the Aztec empire, came to denote "traitor" and "treason" in Mexico and how the Chicana women writers of the Mexican-American ethnic minority north of the American border have tried to rehabilitate her name "into a powerful poetic medium to query the often conflicting interests of the champions of gender equality and racial equality, and of feminism and ethnic nationalism" (1993, 171).

Or witness how Jam Ismail's hybrid subjectivity gets determined in her nomadic wanderings. In *Jamelie•Jamila Project*, Jam Ismail describes herself as "(b. 1940 hongkong), poet, a.k.a. jamu (bombay), jam (hongkong), jemima (edmonton), dismal (london, england), jan isman (vancouver)" (Hassan n.p.). Highly politicized about cultural subjectivity and being caught in crossfire, Jam has played with notions of naming as central to the race writer's toolbox. Her own camouflage in publishing (try to find, for example, her self-published chapbooks, *from the DICTION AIR* or *Sexions*) is perhaps a response to the betweenness and impossibilities in naming hyphenations.

I discovered this complexity on the other side of trying to hide my name because when I was young I wanted to be more white, not Chinese. I sometimes pick out an old jazz LP from high school days and find my signature spelled "F-r-e-d-o-i-s." It works. French is exotic in western Canada.

THE NAME'S ALL I'VE HAD TO WORK THROUGH.

What I usually get at a counter is the anticipa-

tory pause after I spell out "H." Is that it? Double U AY AYCH? I thought it might be Waugh. *What kind of name is that,* Wah? *Chinese, I say. I'm part Chinese. And she says, boy you could sure fool me. You don't look Chinese at all.*

Some of my New England friends pronounce it Fred War. *One of my teachers in graduate school, a poet from Massachusetts, liked to play around with that phonetic pun in our mythology class. He'd say, during the Vietnam war in the sixties, Wah, you should go to War! We should nuke those Chinks! That's when I decided I'd never be an American* We.

I had to book a plane ticket over the phone in Montreal and when I went to pick it up I noticed they'd made it out in the name of Fred Roy. *The flight attendant even asked if I was related to the Canadiens' goal tender Patrick Roy.*

An Okanagan poet sometimes addresses envelopes to me with a comic strip cutout of some kid yelling a big cloud WAH!

Another Canadian poet, whose books are always alphabetized close to mine at the bottom of the bookshelf, has a line that goes "So. So. So. Ah—to have a name like Wah."

And the junk mail addressed to Fred Wan,

> *Fred* Way, *Fred* Wash, *Fred* Wag, *Fred* What *is always a semiotic treat. The one that really stopped me in my tracks, though, was the Christmas card from a tailor in Hong Kong addressed to Fred* Was (Diamond *169).*

The naming tool can be used to mottle, then. To flaunt. To make trouble. To get in your face.

In her essay on Malinche, Pratt cites the practice of *code-switching* as a tactic that "lays claim to a form of cultural power" (177). Code-switching is the movement between two languages, usually the intentional insertion into the master language of foreign or colloquial terms and phrases that represents "the power to own but not be owned by the dominant language. Aesthetically, code-switching can be a source of great verbal subtlety and grace as speech dances fluidly and strategically back and forth between two languages and two cultural systems" (177). A poem by Scott McFarlane, for example, opens with a rhythmic and subtle adjectival movement:

> *my iyes don't*
> *"look Japanese"*
> *canadian*
>
> *between silky furyu lines*

and tempered steel bushido slash
my batting lashes (46)

This slight intrusion of "foreign" terms into incisive, short lines leads, later in the poem, to a more intensive use of "Japanese" phrases that, in the context of questioning the poet's own hyphenation, recognize the blurred edges of language and culture.

not-to ii-ben
hi-sto-ryu i-zu
na-ra-ti-bu

iyes remember
snow white drift
international
mentality garrisons (48)

As Pratt points out, "Code switching is a rich source of wit, humour, puns, word play, and games of rhythm and rhyme" (177). More importantly, however, it functions as part of hyphen poetics as it helps to locate what I call a "synchronous foreignicity" (*Alley* 38): the ability to remain within an ambivalence without succumbing to the pull of any single culture (resolution, cadence, closure). In other words, code-switching can act to buttress the materialization of the hyphen, an insistence of its presence in foreignicity and between/alongside claims of source, origin, and containment.

The extent to which the hyphen floats just out from the shore can be seen when code-switching indicates a complicity or compromise with the dominant culture. Gloria Anzaldua's poem "To live on the Borderlands means you"—

> *are neither* hispana india negra española
> ni gabacha, eres mestiza, mulata, *half-breed*
> *caught in the crossfire between camps*
> *while carrying all five races on your back*
> *not knowing which sides to turn to, run from*
> *(194–195)*

—offers a short glossary of the English translation of some of the Chicano language. Joy Kogawa's well-known novel about the internment of Japanese-Canadians during World War II, *Obasan*, includes the same apology to the master for her cross-coding of Japanese terms. Such deference, in the form of a glossary, has drawn a contentious response from younger writers who see it as "cow-towing" to the mainstream. Code-switching is an ambiguous site for the bilingual writer since it is usually not an assaultive strategy but more a desire to synchronize two or more cultures. But these glosses are frequently the result of editorial advice or insistence, and it is often the publishing industry that is assaultive, that seeks to appropriate or melt such difference into a consumable item.[2]

[2] Roy Miki's essay "Asiancy: Making Space for Asian Canadian Writing" provides both an excellent analysis of the critical reception of Kogawa's novel as well as an insightful note on the "compromise and

A cross-coding with more trajectory, it seems to me, comes from a less deferential diffusion of foreignicity, as in Rajinderpal Pal's poem "apna sangeet":

> *watched the crimson sunset on the thar desert, wrote you love poems that i never showed you. wrote in broken english, spoke in broken hindi, thought in broken gestures you never understood. not apna sangeet but our song, ours and hours alone, wanted you alone in black and gold silk sari with a red bindi in the middle of your forehead, the third eye supposed to give your soul sight, make you understand, cross cultures (39).*

Or sometimes the sensitivity to the need to generate a new "contact" language can lead writers like Sujata Bhatt to com-

---

appropriation" of a recently published anthology of *Many-Mouthed Birds: Contemporary Writing by Chinese Canadians:* "The old truism, 'you can't tell a book from its cover,' may once have been true, but in this design-obsessed consumerist era, the cover is often a tell-tale sign of power relations, stereotypes, and expectations. The cover of *Many-Mouthed Birds*, the dressing for the anthology, becomes a revealing text of the interface between a minority community and the sociocultural majority. It is the face that strikes the (potential) reader immediately: the exotic 'Asian' soft-featured feminized male face, appearing out of the dark enclosure of bamboo leaves. . . . The cover invites the reader in to eavesdrop, to become a kind of voyeur—to listen in on the foreign, the effeminate 'Asian' of western fantasies" (119–20).

pound a title like *Brunizem* from French and Russian for one of her books. The dust-jacket situates the hybrid-hyphen context: "*Brunizem* refers to the dark brown prairie soil of a kind found in Asia, Europe, and North America, the three very different worlds of Sujata Bhatt's imagination. Half the poems are about the East (India); the rest are about the Western world . . . Her mother tongue is Gujarati, and though she writes in English, some of the poems draw directly on Gujarati." Here's a stanza from the title poem that also illustrates that awareness of "naming" I noted above:

The other night
I dreamt English
was my middle name.
And I cried, telling my mother
"I don't want English
to be my middle name.
Can't you change it to something else?"
"Go read the dictionary." She said (105).

The roots of such linguistic attention as cross-coding come, for some writers, from a sense of the hyphen as a locatable place, an *ethnos* otherwise unavailable due to migration. In an essay explaining her own "nomad" poetics, Yasmin Ladha says:

For me, home is a dictionary word. A hard word

I tend to forget. But I do have a home. It exists in my re-departures. My language stems from a layering and matting of words, images, songs, folk stories, from a myriad of places; layering Indian thumri *in a* Kudoki *ballad; Trudeau's red rose in the pink city of Jaipur; plump Shiv* lingum *cresting Crowsnest Mountain in Bellevue, Alberta . . . Often my language has a physical hyphen which is not a border-restraint between words but a trans-evoker, arousing a collective energy from a double or triple hyphen. The hyphen is an extension of my identity, home (6).*

These diasporic writing tactics, though interventionist, still participate in an ethnic/ethic paradigm of "setting it right"—in this case, setting otherness "right." So the elusive migrational floating carpet hyphen offers a literal "place" where the racialized writer can define her own occupancy of this "no-man's land." Trinh T. Minh-ha helps to qualify this site:

Not quite the Same, not quite the Other, she stands in that undetermined threshold place where she constantly drifts in and out. Undercutting the inside/outside opposition, her intervention is necessarily that of both a deceptive insider and deceptive outsider. She is this

> *Inappropriate Other/Same who moves about with always at least two/four gestures: that of affirming "I am like you" while persisting in her difference; and that of reminding "I am different" while unsettling every definition of otherness arrived at (74).*

In order to apply pressure and presence to whatever external investments claim the hyphenated site, however, these nomadic gestures must unceasingly attempt to "deterritorialize" (Deleuze and Guattari, "Minor" 59) the (textual) space through the use of evasive language.

> *For the unitary voice of command is interrupted by questions that arise from these heterogeneous sites and circuits of power which, though momentarily "fixed" in the authoritative alignment of subjects, must continually be represented in the production of terror or fear—the paranoid threat from the hybrid is finally uncontainable because it breaks down the symmetry and duality of self/Other, inside/outside. In the productivity of power, the boundaries of authority—its reality effects—are always besieged by "the other scene" of fixations and phantoms (Bhabha 177).*

In other words, in the process of deterritorializing the dominant properties, say, by code-switching or asking questions, the site of the hyphen being constructed as a possible *ethos* (an ethic, a rightness) is seen as threatening, thus wrong, thus contaminated, polluted. Carol Camper, in her introduction to the anthology *Miscegenation Blues*, unpacks the "stereotype of mixed race women [as] that of moral and sexual degeneracy."

> *It is as if our basic degeneracy as women of colour is magnified by White ancestry. Our so called "Whiteness" increases our "beauty" along with our awareness of it, driving us to a frenzy of bitter abandon so agreeable and piquant to our White male pursuers. It is this particular stereotype that affects our understanding of the word miscegenation itself. Literally this word means, simply, "mixed marriage" and "mixed race," the prefix "*misc,*" meaning mixed. Post-emancipation fear, outrage, and racism in Whites resulted in anti-miscegenation laws in the United States. Other countries such as South Africa, have also had such laws. Not only were miscegenates abominations, but the word miscegenate became virtually synonymous with degenerate. This negative aspect still affects understanding of the word. I had assumed that*

the prefix was "mis," which would indicate "error" or "wrong," relating its meaning to the idea that we could not exist (xxi).

The questions underlying this racism operate in both directions and point to an important aspect of half-bred poetics. In a poem entitled "Sorry, Our Translator's Out Sick Today," A. Nicole Bandy pivots on the interrogative relationship of Black, Indian, and white:

YOU
ask me questions
and won't believe the answers.

Did you ever think that
maybe I get tired of translating? (in Camper 8)

The contradictions, paradoxes, and assumptions active at the hyphen, all indicate a position and a process that are central to any poetics of opposition (feminist, sexual, racial) and that is the poetics of the "trans-," methods of translation, transference, transition, transposition, or poetics that speaks of the awareness and use of any means of occupying a site that is continually being magnetized. How to pass through without being appropriated. "Look both ways for Trains," a sign that became for one of my student's[3] tired eyes after a class on translation theory, "Look both way for Trans." How true her

[3] Susan Holbrook.

mis-seeing was to a condition, a position, a stance towards process and praxis. This is not simply the burden of indeterminate subjectivity as in the nomadic confusion described in Jam Ismail's "ratio quality" (Hassan n.p.), or the silt-like pressure-chamber of cultural purity troubling Michele Chai's poem:

> Don't
> *ask me*
> *to choose between you*
> *Caribbean*
> *Blue (Red)*
>   *Yellow (White)*
>   *Black (Black)*
> . . .
> *I will not choose*
> *between you.* (in Camper 19)

The paradigm of *trans* poetics, whatever its oppositional impetus, situates the writer in an aperture (to extend Bhabha's metaphor of "negative transparency") that offers a greater depth of field, a wide-angle lens that permits distortion at the edges. Though this vantage has been honed through a popular modernist and post-modernist awareness of disruptive and subversive manipulations in morphology, syntax, and meaning, the most significant aspect of these dynamics is in how to maintain the levitation.

A primary inclination for the hyphen, as part of this *trans* (levitational) poetics, is to locate and indicate the blank space, both to preserve and perpetuate the passage position as well as to problematize it so that it doesn't become static. Or, for some writers in Canada, for example, there is the seen need to resist the stasis of identity many European hyphenated Canadians have experienced as "ethnic." My colleague, the "Dutch hyphen Canadian" writer Aritha van Herk, feels "frozen" by "the ethnic tag, the hyphenated definition," and calls for rebellion against the convenient and official multicultural label (1992, 38).

This resistance becomes actualized in a number of formal and semiological ways. It can be visual and asyntactic, as in Annharte's poem "Emilia   I Shoulda Said Something Political":

> *want explanations   make it right for others be a non*
> *statistic   be understood in the marketplace*
> *let's for once inside you let that jaguar purr   asleep she*
> *shifts leg but inside growl   deep I hear it compañera*
> *growl dark like me (Camper 181)*

Or consider Claire Harris' use of the gap in "A Grammar of the Heart" where she questions "How here to say the unsayable" (54):

> *Where i have seen her   a wet snow falling*
> *arms wrapped around her shoulders*
> *rocking   as she may once have rocked away*
> *noonday sun*

And i have seen her make   from the space
between   a new world of snow
and difficult daughters

Once she said   a woman's choice limited
must be quick   and sure
her silences grew baroque (62)

Silence, in fact, becomes part of the grammar, as in Dionne Brand's prose poem sequence, "No Language is Neutral":

Silence done curse god and beauty here,
people does hear things this heliconia peace
a morphology of rolling chain and copper gong
now shape this twang, falsettos of whip and air
rudiment this grammar. Take what I tell you. When
these barracks held slaves between their stone
halters, talking was left for night and hush was idiom
and hot core (23).

Similarly, Kyo Maclear's location of the landscape of word-silence in her poem "The Walls Between Us Are Paper Thin" reveals the complications and ambivalence of the mapping:

silence
hanging heavy
like a net

a twinelike suspension
to entangle to bind to protect

eyes brush flesh
gestures of form
that falter and slip
with each uncharted movement

searching for clues in this journey
mapless yet necessary (Maclear 225)

Or, for a full and ironic treatment of a hybrid silence, read Marlene Nourbese Philip's *Looking for Livingstone: An Odyssey of Silence.*

Though some don't even write it out but try to erase its mediation (see, for example, Michael Ondaatje's *Running in the Family* which attracts, simply, the dust-jacket qualification that it is "exotic"), the hybrid writer usually stands on one side of the tracks, looking "both ways for *trans*," writing through a complicated net of possibilities, the "contact zone," as I do in my poem "High (briti) Tea":

> *How voice the silent dash? Say blindfold, hinge, thorn, spike, rope, slash. Tight as a knot in binder-twine. Faint hope. Legally bound (not just the feet), "Exclusion Act," head tax, railway car to an internment camp, non-status outskirts of town nomad other side of tracks no*

track. Mi-nus mark, not equal sign. A shadow, a fragile particle of ash, a residue of ghost bone down the creek without abridge for the elusive unacknowledged "im" of migratory tongue some cheek to trespass kick the gate the door the either/or, the lottery and the laundry mark, the double mirror, the link between. How float this sign, this agent of the stand-in. Caboose it loose and let it go, it's "Not in Service" anymore.

I'll idle, for now, with Mary Louise Pratt's description of the "contact zone," an accurate characterization of the activity and dynamics of the site of the hyphen for half-bred poetics as well as one that bespeaks hope and possibility:

> *the space of colonial encounters, the space in which peoples geographically and historically separated come into contact with each other and establish ongoing relations, usually involving conditions of coercion, radical inequality, and intractable conflict . . . By using the term "contact," I aim to foreground the interactive, improvisational dimensions of colonial encounters so easily ignored or suppressed by diffusionist accounts of conquest and domination. A "contact" perspective emphasizes how subjects*

are constituted in and by their relations among colonizers and colonized . . . not in terms of separateness or apartheid, but in terms of copresence, interaction, interlocking understandings and practices, often within radically asymmetrical relations of power (Imperial 6–7).

Interview with Ashok Mathur

Ashok Mathur: You refer to *Diamond Grill* as a "biotext." How is this different (or not) for you from what is otherwise referred to as "autobiography" or "life writing?

Fred Wah: I'm using the term "biotext" as a hedge against the kind of writing I do in *Diamond Grill* being hijacked by ready-made generic expectations, the cachet exuded, at least for me, by those other two terms, autobiography and life writing. As I neared finishing with the text, however, I felt I needed to call the hedge a hedge and so I tinted it as "biofiction." For this book, that feels like a happier term, compositionally, since it indicates the possible brush with certain narrative tropes. How to depoeticize the anecdote by claiming its artificiality, and thereby gaining some levitation for the "biotext," feels comfortably aligned with a poetic of drunken tai chi (negative capability and so forth) and my interest in keeping the hyphen hyphenated; *Diamond Grill* settles nothing (I hope).

Mathur: *Diamond Grill* has been touted not only as your first full-length published prose work, but as a departure from your earlier, so-called language-centered, poetry. What is your response to such readings?

WAH: Well, that's true, isn't it? The writing, as prose, was actually spurred along by bpNichol challenging me to open up to other stylistic possibilities, particularly prose, which I had been intimidated by, didn't trust, I suppose, its master position. On the other hand, the prose is also a continuation of the prose poem that started germinating for me as far back as *Breathin' My Name With a Sigh* (1981). The prose poem became more necessary as, through the eighties, my father's visage pursued my writing into a layering of race and identity previously unacknowledged. It has something to do with that stupid notion that prose is talk; for some cathartic reason, nearly fifteen years after his death, I finally gave myself permission to talk to my father, to talk through thinking and memory and the imagination into sentences, saying, story, picture, anecdote. Of course, every once in awhile in *Diamond Grill,* I try to remind the reader that this is still a language event.

MATHUR: This text is comprised of over one hundred prose segments, ranging in length from perhaps half a page to, at most, about three pages. Each prose segment functions in what I'd call a distinct and independent yet enmeshed, interdependent fashion. How do you feel narrative or narrative drive functions in this text?

WAH: Poetry teaches weaving by tonal iteration; the long poem form uses such devices as repetition of linguistic segments that become narrative by accretion. The novel uses narrative differently, to shape a text by delineation and containment. In this biofiction I try to suggest narrative through intertextuality with some of my earlier poems, image and photographic fragments, and clips and anecdotes out of nostalgia and memory. But I don't want the narrative to feel too settled and defined.

MATHUR: There is a great deal of humour in this text, noted particularly when you read it aloud, but there's also a sense of sorrow, sometimes anger, through the text. Do you feel this is what's going in *Diamond Grill*?

WAH: I started the writing in order to confront some of my own anger. I catch myself as an angry person at times, and I wanted to write around inside that anger for some focus for myself. And it's not just racial anger, though that's a volatile site sure enough. But also, as you say, some sorrow, sadness at the past, at the way people have been treated, particularly some of the women in my family's history, heartstrings of memory. Humour sometimes seems the only way of cushioning and sharing such stories.

MATHUR: The epigraph to *Diamond Grill* is a line from *Waiting for Saskatchewan*: "When you're not 'pure' you make it up." The context of this line makes reference to both a Chinese-Canadian history and concepts of mixed race. What do you think *Diamond Grill* offers such communities?

WAH: That's a huge question and I can't offer a pat answer. Certainly some people of mixed race enjoy a considerable identification with the book because, I imagine, the betweenness is not a position that often escapes being hijacked by the angst of purity on either side of it. I try hard in *Diamond Grill*, to foreground the dynamics of the hyphen itself, since, because of that marker,

I've never felt comfortable claiming either the Chinese part or the Canadian part. And Chinese-Canadians are no longer a tangible community, if they have ever been. I suppose, in that sense, the book might offer a little history, some reminders of that early Chinese-Canadian context of the small-town cafes that were everywhere, at least throughout western Canada, so that the considerable sense of community, European or not, in many of these places might be sustained by such a book.

MATHUR: I'm thinking of two passages in particular. This is how the first one begins: "Until Mary McNutter calls me a chink I'm not one. That's in elementary school. Later, I don't have to be because I don't look like one" (72). In the second section the narrator remembers a childhood episode of talking back to an adult which elicits his father's anger: "I get a good talking to about how I can't fool around out there when my father's a businessman, a Chinese businessman, and I'd better not talk back like I did today, to anyone, particularly when they're white, because it all comes down on him, my father, and our family has to be careful in this town" (101).

The first quotation seems to enact Althusser's concept of interpellating the subject, particularly in a racial context. When the narrator is "hailed" as a "chink," he becomes one. The second quotation complicates this further in that the father brings to the forefront his own racialization and the danger implicit in that. My question is about the negotiation in this text with what I would call a racialized space: does being of mixed race (however that's interpreted) create a kind of shifting race identification? To put it in different words, does the mixed-race subject approach a stable racial identity which can never be reached?

WAH: Yes and No. In the section "Sitkum Dollah" I try to suggest a generational transing of the Chinook term "high muckamuck," from its origins through my grandfather, father, and mother. Racialized spaces in my family seem to have occurred similarly. That is, my grandfather likely didn't have to be a "chink" until he was called one. My father, being of mixed race, was undoubtedly more familiar with the instability, the shifting, of racial identity as he was racially slurred in China and in Canada. I'm sure he desired a more stable racial space (don't we all?) but had witnessed the destabilization of sure identities throughout his life, particularly in the descriptive containment of the Chinese in Canada. The racialized space certainly seems to me to be specific to history and person. Race in North America can be modified, to a degree, through class. This is even more possible for a mixed-race person (portrayed nicely in James Weldon Johnson's *Autobiography of an Ex-Colored Man*). The reality of the formula, though, is surely the whiter you are the more class you have. So no, identity is never pure, never sure. And in that the hybrid has as much possibility of "a" sure racial identity as anyone; the only thing sure about it, however, is, as you suggest, that it's always shifting. The sureness of shifting. Thanks to Mary McNutter I not only know who she thinks I am but I know immediately the space she has cleared for both of us is exclusive, surprising, and volatile.

MATHUR: Anger, humour, and self-naming. On page 72, the narrator speaks of his anger both explicitly, through content ("so much anger welled up in me"; "totally enraged") and in the form taken by the prose, running on pell-mell. On page 105, the narrator, now a father himself, gets angry at his child's failure to perform well in school. In the midst of this, there is this line: "Wah! I hit the roof." "Wah!" is an utterance of anger, of self- and family-naming, and perhaps another type of interpellation: calling oneself into being. And on page 169, there's that whole comical bit about the various misreadings and disbeliefs around the name "Wah," particularly as it's attached to the narrator's body. So, my question here is whether the humour (in life, writing, thinking) is a response to a relief from dealing with anger. And, on a more difficult note, is it a combination of these so-called "emotive qualities" that produces what is almost an improvisational quality to this book?

WAH: Again, yes and no. Writing into anger, for me, has been revealing. When I began the book I thought the anger would be racial. The first problem I ran into with that attitude was that the institution of race started to appropriate my anger into its own arguments, its own language. So I soon let that thematic drift downstream, albeit on a long line with the hook still baited. The humour seems partly cathartic and partly improvisational. I mean, no, I don't think the "emotive qualities" produce improvisation. Almost the reverse. For me, improvisation helped reveal the layering of different kinds of anger and their complications. Reel it in, let it out a bit, fish around without preclusion. I've improvised around my name since *Breathin' My Name With a Sigh* and when I do that it reveals to me the complementarity of emotion and humour. Pretty stock stuff. Though I've always used improv as a way of seeing, and to see that anger hook floating, partly hidden, downstream lets me play it through a wider and more generative range of possibilities.

MATHUR: I want to end where the book ends, on the last page. Here you paint a word-image that is somewhere between a memory clip and a still photograph. (I say this because next to the fluidity of the character driving, parking, climbing are some incredibly static and provocative images, the smoky glass, the metal grill, the bodycheck which jars open the door.) So here is my final question: the book ends with a contrasting of "the muffled winter outside and the silence of the warm and waiting kitchen inside," the exterior and interior connected (or is that separated?) by the clanging and rattling of the door, a sound you write as "a noisy hyphen." Hyphens are crucial to you in this text, and I'm wondering how you see them working for or against your writing and where you think the concept of the hyphen takes writing.

WAH: For me, the hyphen is a recent discovery. I've only really come to it in this book. Its dynamics, its conceptual profile, its literalness, is provocative. What a large question "inbetweenness" is. Everything that surrounds our thinking about the hyphen seems suited to my interest in composing language. Its marginalized position (and I don't mean only racially), its noisy—sometimes transparent, sometimes opaque—space feels nurturing. Its coalitional and mediating potentiality offers real engagement, not as a centre but as a provocateur of flux, floating, fleeting.

Theresa Cha offers a wonderfully accurate sense in *Dictee*: "You are moving inside. Inside the stillness. Its slowness makes almost imperceptible the movement. Pauses. Pauses hardly rest. New movement, ending only to extend into the next movement" (51). The idea of an exterior/interior being connected or separated privileges the extremities; I want that "noisy hyphen" of a door clanging and rattling the measure of such movement.

Strangle Four

Say "Sheh!" to get up from the log then get lost and put into cadence the synchronous foreignicity of zone in order to track your own ladder of exhaust swim into the next story some starving elephant as the imperial slacking of alterity just such a gap in trans to collate the terra *of possibility except for being frightened by hunting this dispersal of planned punctuation will rob the arrow of its feather the dart of its you.*

When I assembled *Owners Manual* I thought I had included a poem titled "How to Get Lost." I was surprised, when the book came out, that it wasn't there. I was sure I had included it. Had Daphne Marlatt, the editor, misplaced it? Had I lost it? For years after, I wondered about it until, one day, it tumbled out of some old folders.

Later
the arrow
of hunger

points
back and back
to just tangled
memory
then stop you
are the only
traffic
one trail
crosses another
sticks
are not
complete thoughts
when a stone says
"pick me up"
don't listen
you need to hear
something new.

The plan is to get out of the woods, cadence the event. Circle and project complete. At least that's the lyric zone that confirms the plan. But when the reader feels lost within what seems to be a hermetically sealed maze (such as these "Strangles"), is it enough to know this is, after all, unknown territory and the point is to pay attention to the possible, albeit traumatic, realization of something else? This gap between map and motion sometimes requires subversion and complication in order to reconfigure the terrain into possibility.

The moment is stopped and that requires action and insists on being voiced, even though one might fear a shift from the quiet sitting position to the forces of navigation and their necessary paradigms of anticipation, estimation, and trial. The synchrony of estrangement, the unknown, and mapping could be as simple as climbing a ladder in order to learn how to swim. This is, of course, a privileged style of movement since it assumes stability and the simple can be seen as a gridlock that excludes the external, starves the senses. According to the map we should be there by now. Wherever potential openings can be located intention is reminded of its uncertainty and at the same time gains new guidance systems.

In most writing the plan is the sentence that intends to complete thought. This is a simple sentence. Period. But if it can't move perception outside of its own logic, then the writer is robbed of other possibilities.

Myung Mi Kim's *Under Flag* (1991) locates just such a confliction, the shifting dynamics of a Korean-American contamination. Her writing insists on the sentence or phrase fragment as a unit of frictional movement with the bare and clean precision of minimal punctuation and lots of page space. There is precision on the word as well: tone leading and objectivist concretion.

> *"In my country" preface to the immigrant's fallow*
>
> *Field my country ash in water follow*
>
> *Descent   slur   vowel (26).*

One of the strongest poems in her book, in terms of complicating the hyphenated tongue, is "Into Such Assembly," a playful and reflective dialogue on learning ESL.

And with distance traveled, as part of it
How often when it rains here does it rain there?
One gives over to a language and then
What was given, given over? (30)

Kim's negotiations with language and culture in these poems are resonant with a kind of "re-" poetics that is incisive in how it cuts into memory and image to recuperate, recover, and, especially, re-insist on the presence of the terms (literally) of contact. Her last line in the book, "(Upahead) vision version nor bees neither honey" (46), is, like most of the writing in the book, unpunctuated, yet punctuates intention with a different kind of argument.

The foreign is synchronic with the familiar. As an ecosystem, Korea's DMZ (demilitarized zone), after half a century as no-man's-land, is, apparently, pristine.

The park sign: "Take only memories. Leave only footprints." Take it and/or leave it. The take and leave habit will only starve the elephants, interrupt a mammal presence with absences, forgetfulness, and substitution: no bees, no honey, just you and your dart.

Speak My Language: Racing the Lyric Poetic

The lyric, that is the recognizable and common subject-centered poem, offers a complicated site of practice for most poets. Who is speaking and who is spoken in a poem qualifies a range of compositional stances and boundaries that invariably position writer and reader as either inside or outside the familiar norms and forms of speaking in a poem. Racing the subjectified voice means to use it or rough it up.

This split option, political for sure, has materialized throughout my writing life. It came up strong for me in an early eighties panel on "Writing in Revolution" with Margaret Randall (fresh from Nicaragua with collections of Sandinista women's stories told straight so the people would understand) and Nicole Brossard (fresh from Québécois lesbian-feminist wars with the paterfamilias linguistica), Randall saying the revolution will succeed on the common tongue of the people and Brossard saying there will be no revolution until that (male-based) common tongue is troubled into change. Since then the range of political possibility in poetic language has pretty much dwelled between those two poles. I know which one I opt for but I'm always a little bothered by those race writers who go for the other, that seemingly solid lyric subject ground I can't trust. I can't trust it since, for many of my generation, racing the lyric entailed racing against it; erasing it in order to subvert the restrictions of a dominating and centralizing aesthetic. Yet I'm interested in how the colouring of the negotiations, with whatever thread of the inherited lyric, has consequences for a socially informed poetics (not a politics of identity but a praxis in language). Many of a younger generation of writers have had a not entirely comfortable choice. The polarization of a poetics of resistance and a poetics of accommodation that I have been familiar with isn't a delineation necessarily attractive for some younger writers. Social and cultural production has, in recent years, appropriated the figure of the racialized writer as a measure of containment and control. Thus, the praxis of a lyric poetic within the polarization I'm accustomed to has become somewhat reconfigured as cultural practice, discoursed into notions of production and consumption.

For example, Evelyn Lau, an outspoken opponent of politicizing race, has been fashioned as a "runaway" adolescent (ironically running from an "old world" Asian family into the arms of a new world "multicultural" family), erotic and rebellious Chinese-Canadian. Even though Lau's writing that Walter Lew selected for his anthology of Asian North American writing, *Premonitions*, uses the prose poem stanzagraph (which is why I suspect he chose these pieces over other, more formally normative poems), there is little of the advantage of syntactic disruption and unpredictability that the genre offers. Rather, we are firmly encoded in our reading into the unquestioned substance of a lyric subject paradoxically talking about "breaking through," but contained in a language that guarantees the walls of a familiar prose syntax (in this case, the paragraph) will hold.

> *Hurt me, I say. The room washes somewhere between darkness and light, on the verge of breaking through. I want to break through, live on the side of light, the gathering voices, father, mother, home. As your fingers wring out oxygen I think I hear the voices calling, the walls bang together as if in a storm and the dark closes in (Lau in Lew 138).*

Lau's use of a recognizable specular "voice" that mirrors its predictable gaze is certainly not unique. According to the dust-jackets of her books, she speaks with some rage against social hypocrisy. As her own journalistic performances attest, the degree to which such rage becomes totalized by the codes in which it is written is obvious in the production and use of her "Asian" voice to diffuse and divide the race debate. That is, the subsumed lyric "I" continues, in Lau's case, to function as it's supposed to, within a symbolic order that demands subjection.

This assumed and inherited lyric poetic is practised by other writers in Lew's anthology, but his collection also seeks consciously to drive a wedge into lyric's monism. Lew speaks of "diversity" in his editorial comments.

> *Previous anthologies have been either too small or conservative to convey the astonish-*

> *ing diversity and eloquence of new poetries spread out among numerous networks and poetics—both esoteric and activist, imagist and deconstructive, pidgin and purist, diasporic and Americanist, high literary and pop cultural (575).*

In other words, Lew is highly conscious of disassembling the normative frame which usually houses the lyric to make space for trespass and its necessary innovations.

Brian Kim Stefans's prose poem, one that by chance resonates with the content of Lau's piece, registers an intrusion into the syntactically privileged and spoken "I" of the paragraph by using a run-on (run-over) sentence to resist the sureness of the centre the lyric "I" demands.

> *I can't get you out of my mind though you are so near my heart my spotted elfin an academy of tears stands before you though we have not yet begun to incite the shimmering of your visage when you disappear down an uncharted corridor and become enamel. For the fancy dresses and balls mean nothing to me the crinolines and bagpipes murderous calamities and foods that make you a man nor even the scholarships to health provided you not be there my lone consideration incredible virtue*

that you are. I mean nothing in the failing light
of my incestuous macabre can ever replace you
though there are a mother's promises oh please
come back (Stefans in Lew 539).

This text both pushes against the centralizing magnetism of a controlling speaker and complicates the spoken in a fragmentary collage of objects and voice. The apostrophic "oh" at the end seems ironic alongside Lau's formulaic "I say." Different poetics and different politics? Stefans is the editor of *Arras*, a journal of radical poetry and fiction. He is also mixed-blood, if that makes any difference.

The question of choice within these different poetics and different politics begs some consideration. An argument in defence of Lau's poetics could be made along the lines of a necessary mimesis of the other. A racialized poetics might, for some writers, necessitate the adoption of the dominant form of poetic "speaking" as a way of securing some platform of stability and complicity with power, or, as the case may be, as a critical ironizing. Dionne Brand, a black Carribean-Canadian poet with an identifiable innovative compositional technique, has, for example, teamed up with the formally conventional Adrienne Rich to collaborate on a movie about poetry and politics. Race, and its complications through whiteness, as Michael Taussig reminds us, is as susceptible to "the mischief of reality's sensate skin to both actualize and break down, to say nothing of superseding universals" (144). The extent to which Lau's and Brand's use of the mimetic is mischievous perhaps needs to be scrutinized.

A more interesting and obviously self-conscious location of mischief in the lyric is Theresa Hak Kyung Cha's *Dictee*. Again, Walter Lew has been instrumental in foregrounding this important text in both the anthology *Premonitions* and his own critical collage, *Dikte*. Cha's *Dictee* is a panoramic biotext of nation, race, and identity that explores a wide range of compositional possibilities as a way of confronting precisely who or what does speak from behind History's and Language's constructions. This book quite clearly takes on the containment of inherited form and knowledge through a mimetic portrayal of, as Taussig colours it, the Golden Bough. Cha organizes her text through a contestatory use of the classical western muses. All the muses are there except, as Shelley Wong points out, Euterpe, the muse of Music. Cha substitutes a muse she names (sarcastically?) "Elitere," the muse of Lyric Poetry. Wong's argument is that Cha does this as a means to critique the place of epic.

> *From the profane ground of the personal writing self, Cha proceeds to call down that which is deemed sacred and sacrosanct; the patriarchal cast of the western epic tradition; the religious colonization of Korea; the male-centered narrative of Korean nationalism; monumentalist historiography. . . . In using the lyric moment to critique the epic, Cha is not, however, looking to install the lyric as the preeminent mode of an*

> *oppositional poetics. To the contrary,* Dictee's *insistence on multiple subjectivities would seem to contradict any effort to enshrine a mode of literary production traditionally premised on a single, unified, autonomous consciousness or identity—that of the lyric "I" (117).*

Thus in a section of a book camouflaged as "lyric poetry," we are hard put to find a pronoun. A few "you's" and "*vu*'s" (French is used as a *punctum* in several ways in the book), but no transparent voiceness speaking its curtain of control over the language of the poem. Instead, Cha weaves rhythmically through the resonance of "*aller*" and "*retour*": "She mimicks (sic) the speaking," as she says at the start of her book. She performs mischievous and unfaithful dictation and translation (see Wong 118–119). The words are dead from disuse, Cha chides as she puns through her female speaker "*diseuse.*"

> *If words are to be uttered, they would be from behind the partition, Unaccountable is distance, time to transport from this present minute.*
>
> *If words are to be sounded, impress through the partition in ever slight measure to the other side the other signature the other hearing the other speech the other grasp.*
>
> . . .

If within its white shadow-shroud, all stain should
vanish, all past all memory of having been cast,
left, through the absolution and power of
these words.
Covering. Draping. Clothing. Sheathe. Shroud.
Superimpose. Overlay. Screen.
Conceal. Ambush.
Disguise. Cache. Mask. Veil.
Obscure. Cloud. Shade. Eclipse. Covert (132).

The form pulses before the mirror of composition, an echo of familiar poetic form, trying itself on, turning this way and that, unsettling the sureness of the poem's habit to situate itself behind the authenticity and authority of the poem's speaking "I." It is the assaulted colonized subject who is spoken in this poem .

Throughout *Dictee* we are treated to a continual shifting between prose and lineated poem. The unexpected changes are quite constructive, since the prose poem has become the device of choice for writers who wish to complicate the authority that marginalizes voice. Even writers like Lau, who avowedly avoid oppositional poetics, now utilize the substance of the prose poem as an avant-garde makeup. It has become one of the most popular methods of signalling an unsettling intent and content. Yet even within the variety and range of innovative prose style, the lyric subject can only be troubled so much.

One of the most inventive and playful prose poem writers I know of is Jam Ismail. Jam's a mix—Chinese, Muslim,

Indian, somewhat of a Pound scholar, half the year in Vancouver, half in Hong Kong, and so forth. One of her self-publications is *from the DICTION AIR*, a fascinating lyric and narrative text playing on dictionary entries that she qualifies, in her afterword, in a manner that's similar to Cha's confrontation with the culture bosses:

> *i like to sweep the flat before i settle down to work. the lines of a page of dictionary often remind me of the lines of dust that never get into the pan, they stay on the floor. there are times i feel small dense print (especially the 13 volume* oxford dictionary*) as an arrangement of dust (n.p.).*

Jam is also dexterous in shifting the autobiographical pronoun to the third person and, in a piece titled "(Translit)" she further uses the prose poem's penchant for self-parody to riff on the diasporic nature of identity.

> ***from kid inglish***
>
> *:"didi" meant big sister (bengali), little brother (cantonese), DDT (english). to begin with, inglish had been at home, with cantonese & hindustani. one of the indian languages, the kid felt in bombay. which british hongkong tried to colonize. descended on all sides from the*

> *Idiosyncracy, the kid disdained grammar class, refused to parse, opted to be remote parsee.*
>
> *:at school wrote her first poem,* DAMON NOMAD *(damon nomad). & what mean while was writing her, what* nom de womb? *reverb with '47 (indian, pakistan), '48 (koreas), '49 (chinas, germanies), '54 (vietnams).*
>
> *: "hey," he bellowed, pants down in quebec, "bring in some english mags, i can't shit in french!" claude nearly kicked him in the anglo. macaulay's minute & roosevelt's second unearthed in canadian library digs. chattel feared english had him in its grip. spooken for, pun-ish (46).*

The lyric subject in such writing doesn't disappear. In fact, the conditioning of the writing depends on its "poetic" presence (and distance). The proximity of that romantic autobiographical realism is deflected only momentarily by syntactic and punctuative gestures, what Jeff Derksen calls the thematizing of language.

Yet what is achievable here, I think, and surely not only momentarily for the racialized writer who, like Lau, holds onto the inherited lyric bag, or, like Ismail, punches it, is something of the characterization Paul Smith attributes to Barthes's sense of writing:

> *the process of language's constructing a momentary subjectivity for the human agent who always, by contestatory and resistant use and reception of language, emerges as the place where contradictory discourses are marked (110–111).*

We see the lyric as a confluence of contradictory discourses in Harryette Mullen's poetry. What Henry Louis Gates, Jr. calls the "stunningly lyrical voice" (back cover) of *Muse and Drudge,* Mullen's punning and witty takeoff on "mules and drugs" (74), is an intrusion of "hip hyperbole" (back cover) into both lyric accessories and the fragility of "his master's voice." The accoutrements of lyric are placed up front and in our face as Mullen riffs around the predictable, as well as unpredictable, materiality of the poem:

> *Sapphire's lyre styles*
> *plucked eyebrows*
> *bow lips and legs*
> *whose lives are lonely too*
>
> *my last nerve's lucid music*
> *sure chewed up the juicy fruit*
> *you must don't like my peaches*
> *there's some left on the tree*

you've had my thrills
a reefer a tub of gin
don't mess with me I'm evil
I'm in your sin (1)

The poem shadow-boxes both the lyric "I" and what it's dressed in, unrelenting in its confrontation with form and expectation, with the seemingly absolute presence of "a" poem.

handful of gimme
myself when I am real
how would you know
if you've never tasted (3)
. . .
just as I am I come
knee bent and body bowed
this here's sorrow's home
my body's song
. . .
proceed with abandon
finding yourself where you are
and who you're playing for
what stray companion (80)

Parody, indeterminate logic, extreme playfulness—features that have come to be associated with the prose poem—are here reshuffled back into the lined poem with incisive effect.

Yet some race writers rely on the recognition that the lyric poetic is as negotiable as the social. We might consider, for example, Mullen's acute attention to the social in all of her writing (the streets, the supermarkets, the homeless) as a conscious insertion of class and community into disjunctive poetics in order to wring from it a truer political vantage. Roy Miki's poem "history is we," written in the midst of his activism during the Japanese-Canadian redress negotiations, demonstrates the hesitant and "fear of trust" handshake with the culturally inherited "i" of the lyric, the forced complicity with the vocabulary of surrounding discourses.

fear of trust
& the tongue slides
over the dial

stations of the way
memorabilia to tuck away
where the line gets drawn

single purpose?

the whirlwind tour
the horizon looks
clear up here—

diffidence in the doorway
syllables in the drainage

fine night to be
standing in rain mist

crowds on yonge street
willing over celluloid

instant of what
am I saying
seeing etc etc

re
cognition

& the talk turns on
group vs individual

the cross of burden
i heard said

we is i
in the vocab
we is one

excuse me
i'm patient

the sky again
(blue) sky

& the inching
back home (84–85)

In this "inching" homeward through the artifacts of democracy, tongue sliding over the "diffident . . . syllables . . . [and] vocab" structured around an historically constituted "we," the "i" must be "patient" and bearing, aware of "where the line gets drawn." But can Miki's "re/cognition," even under a blue sky, become the "ignition" such a conscious poetic seeks to enact?

In *Colour. An Issue* Miki and I published a very quick and pushy prose poem by Metis writer Marilyn Dumont. As an editor I was encouraged by what appeared to be an unusually exploratory compositional stance by a native writer. Many of the native writers and writers of colour I've been reading seem caught and contained, like Lau, in the more accessible conventions of the lyric. When Dumont's first book, *A Really Good Brown Girl*, came out, however, I was a little disappointed at even the moderate room given to the confessional or representational. Poems with lines like

> '. . . .
> *When I was five*
> *the yard I played in*
> *had a sky this colour,' I say 'what*
> *colour?' he says (31).*

seem to undercut the stylistic advantages Dumont is capable of in, say, a poem like "Leather and Naughahyde":

> *So, I'm having coffee with this treaty guy from up north and we're laughing at how crazy 'mooniyaw' are in the city and the conversation comes around to where I'm from, as it does in underground languages, in the oblique way it*

> *does to find out someone's status without actually asking, and knowing this, I say I'm Metis like it's an apology and he says, 'mmh,' like he forgives me, like he's got a big heart and mine's pumping diluted blood and his voice has sounded well-fed up till this point, but now it goes thin like he's across the room taking another look and when he returns he's got 'this look,' that says he's leather and I'm naughahyde (58).*

And, stylistically, the book covers a fairly wide range of composition. She uses the page, the line, the anecdote, lots of imagery, and generally covers a number of formal possibilities. So why am I bothered that a young "race" writer should seem so "dilettantish" in her use of the poem, so "un"-intentionally aestheticized and politicized? Could it be, for Dumont, that even the recent avant-garde poetics are as complicit with the hegemonic designs of form as are the more conventional? Could her lack of commitment to a singular poetic project, unlike the mimetic enactments of Lau and Brand, indicate some mistrust? She is, like they are, a careful and intelligent writer. We might consider, here, Elaine Chang's notion of a "Politics of Equivocation." Judith Butler's observation that such ambivalence is a site of agency seems also a useful position to consider.

> *Thus, there is an ambiguity of agency at the site of this decision.... One decides on the condition of an already decided field of language, but this*

repetition does not constitute the decision of the speaking subject as a redundancy. The gap between redundancy and repetition is the space of agency (Butler 1997, 129).

If this is the situation, Dumont, and others like her, would seem to participate in the use of a derivative formal innovation, not in order to trouble a dominant and inherited structure (social or poetic) but to locate an "ordering intervention" (Clark 25) within a poetic that is intrinsically informative. That is, a racialized lyric, caught in the hinges of inherited poetic forms, might adopt an ambiguous regard to both lyric interference and lyric convention in order to recuperate the agency of linguistic choice.

The question that seems to surface here is whether the lyrically constituted speaking and spoken subject that is troublesome for some racialized writers is at all similar to the trouble it is for, say, Ron Silliman or Daphne Marlatt. Just as political? Do we need to examine, in this context, Hiromi Goto's observation that "choice is a position of privilege" (220)? What censorships are constructed in the "turbulences of an omnivorous fiction"?

BELITTLED BY THE TURBULENCES OF AN OMNIVOROUS FICTION—

the harassed 'lyric' faulters in a world of genetic-engineering and multi-national take-overs. an unremittingly, desacralized, human/bio/sphere trembles within its transparent skin. australian aborigine painter/shaman those with x-ray vision will tell you that all living creatures have that kind of see-through-skin and that's why they're depicted with their entrails hanging out. long before i said a single intelligible thing that could be quoted a lullabye cradled a delinquent fear sequestered in the coil of my pillowed ear. . . . the small voice, some would call, 'pipsqueak,' lifts itself up by an act of incomparable, lightness. let its 'etudes' season us with a pinch of salt. let even a flawed lyric speak out, against all that seems, furiously-fated. let a bountiful harvest of sea-weed apparel our naked genitalia. henceforth: the Gods on high will have to save their own faces from our conceits and indiscretion/s . . . un-diminished; the fine thread of an ancient lullabye weaves its way through, my own small thronging/s (Kiyooka, Pacific Windows *295–296).*

Strangle Five

Recognize cousins as those sub-paths of relationship just happening upstream but try to turn that feast into the trace of a biotext that isn't a net or even next September but distinct and personal some kind of syncopation of chronology that bumps heart into the hyphen of chaos no theory or category in these narrows will catch fish for long so what if they get away and critical distance cut by everybody dancing like crazy, eh?

Family is both a container and open to other vectors of recognition that create slight movements in the shadows indicating the relativity of the minute and the particular, the little and the local, without claim to any rationalism or hierarchy, just that possible motion further responsible for the custody of an inhabited intervention.

The semiotic of the family hijacked by production and consumption ideology. Value. Vote for the family party. The lake rose three inches last night. Take out a genome for life. The plan isn't the body, it's the package.

The family in the midst of an always-shifting biotext.

Sudden discontinuities become regular. "The problem [is] to recognize and explore our distrust of system, of grid . . . " (Kroetsch, "For Play" 92).

Question Air: Male, 60s, dad dead 54/1966, mum in her 80s does well, two younger brothers one sister wife two daughters married, Ethnicity and Race? (you are yr father) no "group" Scots/Irish/Swede/Chinese mixed, class? 14 to 8 to 6 hr/days one century up 'n up, north interior rain forest out of prairie and back to foothills, teach and write, sanitation? two bathrooms one septic field forever, housing? used except one, no two, from the ground up, t-shirts cotton desert boots finally a dark suit in case, low-oil vegetarian, stressors? any blip like losing things or bad back, breathing's ok but wake up early every morning genetic cholesterol controlled, resilient from broken ribs but no wars, lost international immunization card in Atlanta Hotel in Bangkok, a few old friends some colleagues, quit smoking at 34 beer and wine, pharmacy multi-v robaxacet viagra melatonin prostease.

As if. But never normal.

Perhaps dancing could be a "magic bullet." A strategy aimed at my very own boundary condition. The dog's ok as long as she's with me.

Bio is useful not only as an imaginary container for the self, like one's name, but also as a means to domesticate hybridity, negotiate the terms of an individual (though dangerously just as consumed) *trait d'union* (I like the trans of "trait" that colours the French hyphen). Difference is minimized and only temporarily deflected.

Louise Bak's *Gingko Kitchen* is an example of the kind of poetry that insists on keeping taut the interrogative elements of such modulated identity. The sustained activity at the level of the syllable in Bak's poetry substantiates that old Olsonian claim to the site of the syllable as the site of intellection, minding mind. Bak's attention to syllabic compounding is intense and carefully meshed for readability. Lines like "in flesh-hold of igneous foulard tied around shuttlecock eyes" syncopate with compressed precision. Her sense of moment-by-moment word detail illuminates the presence of writing-on-the-move.

> *volute across time to great-grandmother's*
> *partitioned corner, debeaking falsely timid*
> *semi-wild turkeys, while wrapping her*
> *bloody hands in thin gossamer threads*
> *noodles oggled from the memory of culinary crones,*
> *driven to believe hongyan boming across bitter*
> *journey. the chest opens emptied of yecao xianhua*
> *(90–91).*

The advantage of this formal attention is a poetry of incredible balance and daring. Each poem becomes a performative tight-rope, a high-wire act that indicates every gesture as minimal and necessary, moving tenaciously from tower to tower, line to line, and even from poem to poem.

Bak demonstrates a finesse with the line as a unit of composition that is acute in its awareness of the concrete and discernible.

the HE(A)Rstories of
lichen-wisp bodies
drifting in Hsiang Kang *harbour*

collop milfoil boys
bundled teary-eyed
at semen-puddle corner (55)

Each line stands as discrete; the economy of movement is precise and the line resonates between the linear action of the words and syllables and isochrony of utterance.

This fine balance operates between the poems as well. The book itself reflects the paratactic effect of the lineal movement in the poems. Though we can read a great variety of image content and verbal play, each poem extends its performance into a choreographed and iterated high-wire act. The physicality of the language is trussed into a material insistence on the sexual and racial body. The exoticized "oriental" female is constituted literal and tangible.

a tsui *world*
where women
are picture-perfect sexual d spensers
wrigglin in s lken paroxysms
for the b nary

refuck expert
facializes laundro-mantic landscape
with Suzie Wong equestrian on Li Hsiao-Lung *(54–55)*

The success here lies in the balance between story and language; the narrative moves in tandem with the concrete foregrounding of the materiality of the words themselves.

Compared to other narrative and poetic treatments of the sexualized and racialized subject in contemporary writing, Bak's poetry offers particular advantages. What it can do that a more transparent and conventional poetic cannot is articulate our complicity with language whenever we use it to formalize a public space for ourselves. *Gingko Kitchen* performs this feat with rivets.

Chinese Avant-Garde Poetry

I spent much of 1995–96 anticipating a government-initiated China/Canada cultural study tour. The tour was set up by Heritage Canada for six Canadian artists of Chinese heritage. I was the only writer in the group and, after several bureaucratically botched attempts to mount the tour, three of us visited China in August 1996. My statement of intent for the selection committee framed my early notions of what I might consider on this study tour:

1. The subject of a Chinese-Canadian hybrid identity has been at the centre of my writing for the past sixteen years. The narrative representation of this project is most accessible in *Waiting for Saskatchewan* (Governor-General's Award for Poetry 1985) where I document a highly personal apprehension of cultural identity, including an early trip to China. This narrative has extended into a prose biofiction (*Diamond Grill*) that figures the Chinese-Canadian cafe as background for interrogating some of the complexities of racialization and hybridity.

2. As part of my study and practice of poetry and poetics, I have been acutely interested in formal innovation in modern and recent Chinese (and other Asian) poetry. I am par-

ticularly interested in the poetry and aesthetics of a contemporary group of writers who call themselves "Original: Chinese Language-Poetry Group" (published in translation by Parataxis Editions, England, 1994). These writers (Che Qianzi, Zhou Yaping, Yi Cun, Hong Liu, Huang Fan, and Xian Meng), mostly in Suzhou and Nanjing, seem to have devised, with some intensity, a discourse and praxis of contemporary writing that might usefully be juxtaposed alongside similar modern and postmodern attentions in English-language poetry writing and critical thinking.

3. As someone who has been writing creatively and critically through the knots of "race" (the ethnopoetic, the nomadic, the exotic, and so forth), I would welcome the opportunity to reflect on western assumptions about "our" imperialist iconography with Chinese artists as well as, obversely, to consider "their" frame of external and foreign possibility for their own work. I would find especially useful for my own practice any dialogue that might clarify the social consciousness and activity that underlies the production of art and writing; the "Originals," for example, through their insistence on the written character, offer useful insights into poetic practice that could enable my own endeavors into language and culture.

4. Since my current writing project problematizes "hybridity," in a more general and, perhaps, obtuse way, this tour could help me untangle ambiguities about my Chinese hyphened (–) identity that I have been focused on in my writing for

the past fifteen years. As well, I would like both to represent some of the complex of Canadian cultural and social hybridity to Chinese artists as a facet of Canadian identity that they are perhaps unaware of and, in contrast, I would find it extremely useful to become more cognizant of attitudes about race and hybridity in China.

Besides focusing on the "Originals" in the Nanjing-Suzhou area, I had also determined the locations of a few more poets through other publications and discussions. A major source of opinion and information was Yunte Huang, a graduate student at the University of Buffalo who had introduced, through the Electronic Poetry Centre's web magazine *Rif/T*, a selection of "Avant-Garde Chinese Poetry" (six poets from 1982 to 1992: Zhou Jingzi, Mo Fei, Mo Mo, Liu Manliu, Men Lang, and Yu Jian) translated and soon to be published by Wang Ping in New York. In both the excerpts from Wang Ping's introduction to her forthcoming collection and in Yunte Huang's notes for *Rif/T*, certain shapes of the contemporary Chinese poetic landscape appeared.

There were the "Misty" poets (Bei Dao and others) who had, since the late sixties, rebelled against the official artistic ideology that the arts must serve politics and the people. The "misties" had attempted to "recover the human self."

Next, the "New Generation" poets pushed against the "Misty" modernist poetics of the aloof and heroic artist and art. As Wang Ping puts it,

The 'new generation' poets are trapped between

their rejection of the Communist ideology and their distaste for the relentless advance of the capitalist mass culture. Facing the threat of losing their identity and subjectivity, they feel an urgent need to find a foothold in a local and global environment which is in constant and rapid transition. To the 'new generation' poets, the misty poets' single-minded belief in truth, perfection, and humanity, and their imagistic, symbolic method for writing poetry are outdated. The most important task now is not to celebrate 'heroism' and utopian idealism, but to strip off the facades of decency, beauty and sublimity [sic] from language and art. The poems of the 'new generation' tend to point to the eternal darkness and ugliness of human nature. The works included in this anthology are characterized by a generalized sensitivity to breaks and discontinuities, to difference rather than identity, to gaps and holes rather then seamless webs, and by an emphasis on re-establishing the 'pure' relationships between words and objects, spatial experience and exploration (Rif/T, n.p.).

Ping's description of these new poets bridges a range of context, narrative, and poetics. The effects of ideological reformation on these poets, at least as it's interpreted here for western readers, is to relocate poetry's attention to language. She cites Yu Jian: "Poetry begins from language and ends with language." As I'll point out, this is echoed, in Zhang Ziqing's preface to *Chinese Language Poetry*.

Wang Ping's use of the language of identity politics to separate the new poets from the Misty poets might be a misleading positioning for western readers. In fact, excluding the Nanjing-Suzhou poets, and Yu Jian in Kunming, many of the new poets seem to have separated themselves from the Misty poets by shifting to highly lyric and confessional modes, despite some of the desire in China to be more grounded in the purities of Chinese language.

Yunte Huang comments that, while Wang Ping's translations are a "noble" effort, her selection ignores "other equally significant experimental poetry groups such as Original poets (based in Suzhou) and Feifei poets (based in Sichuan, n.p.)." Huang's comments also gave me my first inkling that the context of my project should shift to include some attempt to understand the processes of mediation. Huang says:

> *Not only is experimental poetry still marginalized inside China, but the introduction of Chinese poetry in the west has so far been restricted to a very narrow scope. A quick look at the translation anthologies of contemporary Chinese poetry published in the United States in recent years will show that Misty*

> *poetry still dominates the stage of representation. While such a narrow-mindedness in poetry's reception needs a careful investigation for its political and cultural implications, a project such as Wang Ping's will definitely* broaden *the western view of Chinese poetry and bring a new phase to our literary exchange ("Commentary", n.p. emphasis added).*

Another important source of preliminary reading was Yunte Huang's essay, "The Translator's Invisible Hand: The Problems in the Introduction of Contemporary Chinese Poetry." Huang reviews some of the translations of Chinese poetry into English since 1984 and usefully raises questions about the notions of purity and transparency, aurality and originality, in translation. He relates "some translators' formal reduction in their textual rendering to the larger ideological reduction we have encountered in the introduction and reception of contemporary Chinese poetry in the English-speaking world"; he also calls "for a reading which is not simply a self-verification of some crude political interests but is fully committed to the text's inseparable formal and social materiality" (80). In other words, he reminds us, the mediated energies involved in translation are suspect and demand scrutiny. The translation and publication of the so-called "Original" Chinese-language poetry, for example, needs to be read with this in mind.

A few other sources also gave me a hint about what to expect. I'm not sure I entirely agree with Michelle Yeh's thesis, in "The 'Cult of Poetry' in Contemporary China," that "[f]or many avant-garde poets in China today, poetry is not just a private and personal endeavour of a creative and spiritual nature; rather, it is elevated to being the supreme ideal in life and a religious faith" (53). When I asked poets in China what they thought of this notion, they didn't seem to support it very strongly. Their minds appeared more concerned, perhaps, with cultivating an international presence for their poetry than with ordering a more political or ideological frame for their writing within China. However, it's just this kind of complex dealing of a cultural "betweenness" that I am interested in illuminating. Yeh substantiates her arguments through the poems themselves (and she can read and write both languages) so it could be that my resistance to the cultification of poetry has more to do with my own North American preferences for particular cultural envelopes than with her own more familiar knowledge, though she, likewise, invests in a similar institutionalization and North Americanization of foreignicity. In any case, her article proved useful for names and contexts, and I referred to it often in my interviews with Chinese poets.

But I want also to consider her (and others') unexamined use of the term "avant-garde." In Beijing, Xi Chuan handed me a copy of a chapter from a North American dissertation by someone named Zhang Xudong; the title of the chapter is "The 'Avant-garde' Intervention." To be sure, both Zhang Xudong and Michelle Yeh seem to use the term in a general way to mean recent, innovative (but not "modernist") writing. But I wonder if they have considered the particular contamination of that term in western critical discourse to reflect a modernist, almost-exclusively white male and, paradoxically, competitive mainstream agenda. Or perhaps they have: there are hardly any women writers included in the current North American and British canonization of contemporary Chinese poets.

But I doubt it. What is surely going on in this cultural translation is a domestication of foreignicity: the imposition of a descriptive critical terminology that seeks to synchronize an alien production within a familiar "postism" (postmodern, postcolonial) in order to, as Lawrence Venuti might suggest, bring the author home rather than seeking an "ethnodeviant pressure on those values to register" difference by "sending the reader abroad" (210).

This became rather problematic for me in my discussions with most of the poets and particularly with the "Original" poets of Nanjing and Suzhou. And here, perhaps, is a rather sad example of lopsided exchange value in cultural reading (or breeding, depending on how you look at it). Discussions with the "Originals" centred on the publication of *Original: Chinese Language-Poetry Group* because my copy of this anthology was the first the writers had seen of it. Though the anthology had been published and distributed in the west since 1994, the poets themselves had not received copies. I found this matter quite reprehensible and, subsequently, wrote to Drew Milne, the publisher of *Parataxis*, and Jeremy Prynne, the editor of this particular issue, with no response. Indeed, I have since discovered that translations published in western literary magazines frequently appear without the writer's permission or awareness. One might suspect, at least in North America, certain self-aggrandizing uses of this material.

Even prior to going to China I was curious about the designation of the term "language poetry" to the "Original" poets as it almost overlapped with the Chinese translation of "Selected Language Poems by Charles Bernstein, Hank Lazer, and James Sherry" (Ziqing and Huang, *Selected*), three poets who are associated with the original *L=A=N=G=U=A=G=E* magazine in New York. The narrative of this apparently shared identity runs, as far as I can figure out, something like this. Zhang Ziqing, China's leading scholar of American poetry, claims to have introduced American language poetry in lectures in China as early as 1991 (4). Jeff Twitchell, who taught English at Nanjing University around the same time, "translated" (he apparently knew no Chinese, and notes that the translations are "collaborations" primarily with students who worked with him at Nanjing University) six Yangste poets and collected them into a special edition of the British *Parataxis* magazine titled "Original: Chinese Language-Poetry Group." In 1993 Ziqing, at Nanjing University, brought out a slim bilingual volume of work by six other local poets entitled *Chinese Language Poetry* as well as, with Yunte Huang, the above-mentioned bilingual *Selected Language Poems* of Bernstein, Lazer, and Sherry. This interchange of the nomenclature was critiqued and criticized by Leonard Schwartz in an issue of *Talisman*. Schwartz, out of apparent spite for the successful brokering of "language" poetry in his own back yard, is highly critical of its import/export beyond America.

For one thing, the entry of Language Poetry

> *into China at the moment of China's greatest hysteria over "free trade" helps bolster Eliot Weinberger's claim (in* Sulfur *20, 1987) that there is a kind of rapport between the aesthetic of language poetry and the growth of capitalism in which the poetry helps mask the damage that is being done to the culture by the market (173).*

Though this is a rather uninteresting local jockeying for position, part of what he has to say is worth noting, particularly since this "local jockeying for position" can be seen played out in China as well.

Nonetheless, there has been a general swing to an attention to "language" (not "l=a=n=g=u=a=g=e poetry") among most of the "new generation" Chinese poets. Zhang Ziqing sees the members of the Nanjing group as the most firm in their resolve:

> *They sternly claimed that the word is poetry and poetry ends in the word; that is, poetry takes the word as its ultimate end. All poetical meaning is elicited from the language of a poem; language is the everything of the poem: its origin and its bedrock . . . They firmly believe that . . . the Chinese characters conceal the whole history of man's interaction with*

the world, profound philosophical significance and aesthetic value (2–3).

But the Beijing poets voiced their disapproval of "l=a=n=g=u=a=g=e" poetry to me, at least as represented by Zhang and the "Originals." (See my "China Journal"168). Perhaps not so oddly, this reflects similar formal, social, and geographic oppositions in the west. Yu Jian, far off in the southwest in Kunming, whose poetic project is to recuperate the "common" language of the street in order to fend off the intrusion of both communist and western idealism, is a poet who seems to garner the widest interest of the younger generation poets. Yu Jian gave me a copy of some translations of his poetry by the Canadian writer Michael Day. Day's enthusiasm for Yu Jian's poetry, though informed and intelligent, is tainted with a suspect contextualization (of one of Yu Jian's poems) within the modern poetics of Hart Crane and Allen Ginsberg. Such thematizing is, ironically, bound to contain our reading of the translation within what we see as a dominant aesthetic and what Yu Jian sees as a suspect imperialism.

One further aspect of the modernist "avant-garde" that is paralled in China is the paucity of women poets. Of the sixteen poets to be included in Wang Ping's anthology, two are women. Of the six poets published in *Original*, one is Hong Liu (who is now married to Zhou Yaping, another of the "Originals"). She was not particularly forthcoming when I tried to ask her about her writing.

There are, at the same time, innovations in language and form being carried out. Che Qianzi and Zhu Jun, both of the

Nanjing "language" group, have used visual and asyntactic methods to foreground attention to language.

These notes are, admittedly, configured from a rather meagre, touristic, and North American exposure to contemporary Chinese poetry. Poetry's situation in China is much more complicated than I can portray. When I started my "peep" into contemporary Chinese poetry, I had expectations of, as I said above, juxtaposing similarities in formal innovation and modern and postmodern discourse alongside my own. I feel now that such affiliation is, by and large, a skewed and appropriative attention. I started out thinking of rubbing my own hybridity into our exchange and instead discovered that, rather than conflating their work with my own, I need to find means of measure and renovation whereby hybridity (and heterogeneity) can be negotiated as a generative betweenness. "Our" imperialist iconography gets in the way. But so does "their" frame of external and foreign possibility. The cultural economics of this exchange need to be shaken into view. As Roger Lee, the organizer of our tour, kept observing: "China deconstructs, China reconstructs."

Objects of Resistance: An Interview with Hong Kong Poet Leung Ping-Kwan

FRED WAH: Do you write in Chinese?

LEUNG PING-KWAN: Yes, I've always written in Chinese. I've only just begun trying to write in English recently, hoping to address a broader audience and to find new means and venues to express myself. Writing in English, I see the differences between the two languages and I feel a lot more comfortable with Chinese. On the one hand, Chinese is my language. I started using it early in life so I feel very comfortable with it. With Chinese I can take many risks because I know the language well and I'm not afraid of making mistakes. On the other hand, because I've grown up in a colony, English represents something different. For a long time I resisted speaking or writing in English, because psychologically . . .

WAH: A sense of colonization?

LEUNG: Yes. I refused to speak or write in English for much of my past even though I studied foreign literature. I chose to do this because in our society English represented a certain status. Everybody wanted to go into the English Department [to study

English literature] so that after they graduated they could get a better job with the government. English speakers came to represent an elite class in society that would look down upon people who could not speak the language. I resisted that attitude by not using English.

WAH: Was this primarily a class thing then?

LEUNG: Sort of. Eventually, speaking English did become a class thing, but I think its role in Hong Kong was determined by the educational and social organization within the colony. For a lot of university students, if you studied Chinese language and literature you wouldn't get as good a job as you would if you had graduated from the English Department. As well, Hong Kong is a commercial society, so you need English. At an early age, English represented for me either a commercial language or an official language, because that's what you needed to fill out all sorts of forms. Subsequently it represented the attitude of a higher class of people who occupied certain privileged positions. However, by reading creative works—including underground writings—I was able to see other usages of English.

WAH: But hasn't the language of commerce infiltrated Chinese as well?

LEUNG: That's true. From the mainland perspective, the language used in Hong Kong is not pure Chinese; it is contaminated with commercialism. But writing creatively in Chinese is a resistance to its commercialism; and the use of more colloquial Chinese is a type of resistance against the more formal uses of Chinese in mainland China.

WAH: The criticism I heard in mainland China was not so much that Hong Kong Chinese was filled with commercial discourse but that it was archaic.

LEUNG: I can understand that too. Do you know why? Because after 1949, and especially during the Cultural Revolution (1966–76), Chinese classics were criticized on the mainland but continued to be studied in Hong Kong. Historically speaking, since the period after the May Fourth Movement (1919), and in response to the New Literature Movement (1917), and so on, there has been a lot of criticism of classical literature.

WAH: The switch to the vernacular?

LEUNG: Yes. At that point the criticism of the classics was from a cultural perspective and there was a demand for new literature to reach out to the general public. But after 1949, and especially during the Cultural Revolution, literary criticism became linked with the desire for particular political ends. For example, the criticism of the Chou dynasty was actually aimed at Chou En Lai. Therefore, critics used cultural critiques of classical literary texts as a means to attack rival political figures. In fact, the contemporary criticism of Confucianism was a criticism of more traditional, conservative, political forces. So the whole attack on the classics was not actually conducted in an academic or scholarly way, but rather as a political campaign. From 1949 until the beginning of the eighties, the classics were not really accessible to mainland people. Ironically, Hong Kong and Taiwan were the only places that could continue the study of classical Chinese culture.

WAH: I see. So there would be a greater influence of classical Chinese in Hong Kong and Taiwan?

LEUNG: Yes, in spite of the misconception that Hong Kong is a cultural desert. That's why it's so difficult to understand Hong Kong. I can understand perfectly the criticism coming from the mainland perspective because our cultural formations and literary production have been so different.

WAH: So their view of your poetry, although I don't know if they've even read it, would be that it is not very "modern"?

LEUNG: Not exactly, in my case. The overall trend in Hong Kong has been that we have had more opportunity to be in contact with classical Chinese literature. At the same time, on the mainland, the use of the Chinese language has, in a very strange way, been influenced by, for example, the literal and stiff translation of Marxist texts. In my poetry, however, I dialogue with classical Chinese culture but I also escape from the limits of an archaic sense of culture by focusing on modern subjects.

WAH: But there's a very curious phenomenon going on in mainland China right now. This return to the classical in the eighties, the third generation (post-Misty, post-1980) returning to not so much the classical literature, although they do that too, but to the notion of the purity of the originary characters and the demand by all these young poets that, if you're going to be a poet, you have to be steeped in the basics of the Chinese language.

LEUNG: That, exactly, is a reaction to the earlier generation who threw away the classics. But in my personal development, I've tried different kinds of things. I have written a series of poems which are contemporary responses to classical Chinese literature and language. One of the things I'm working on now is a series of poems called "Museum Pieces," which came out of an installation art project. From a contemporary position, I want to create dialogues with old artifacts which represent classical Chinese culture. During the eighties I wrote a book of poems entitled "Lotus Leaves" in which the language is very condensed and complicated. That text is a kind of modern Chinese version of the classical "thing" (*yongwu shi*) poetry, poems about objects. When I first started writing I reacted against the general trend in Taiwan and Hong Kong which, for some, had become a rather slavish adherence to classical embellishment and beauty. So, when I first wrote I became known for the use of conversational language because I wanted to get rid of those classical influences. I was reacting against the general mentality at the time which was not really to understand classical culture but, rather, to use it as a kind of decoration.

WAH: Do you know Yu Jian's poetry? He's another poet who wants to write "thing" poetry and at the same time believes his responsibility to the Chinese written character is very important.

LEUNG: Yes, I met him in Belgium and we exchanged poetry books. I feel a certain affinity to him. As a young poet emerging in the nineties, he seemed to be different from earlier poets like Yang Lian or Bei Dao. Although I started earlier (in the seventies) and in Hong Kong, I feel closer to the younger generation writing in the eighties and nineties in mainland China and in Taiwan. Now when people talk about contemporary Chinese poetry, we should take examples from Hong Kong, Taiwan, and the mainland, and also look at examples from different periods. What has been done in Hong Kong in the seventies, Taiwan in the eighties, and the mainland in the nineties, are particular moments of particular cultural contexts or crises which induce poets to use language to respond to certain things in certain ways. I do see a lot of affinity there but nobody has actually looked at these affinities and differences. In order to understand the richness of contemporary Chinese poetry we should look at these different moments and efforts from different communities.

WAH: But the mainland writers seem to have been very resistant to including Hong Kong and Taiwan in their own reckoning.

LEUNG: I've noticed their exclusion of us in their anthologies and discussions.

WAH: However, Yu Jian was telling me that he was very proud to have entered and won a poetry contest in Taiwan, but he doesn't particularly care for the poets in Taiwan.

LEUNG: What a pity!

WAH: Do you think that your identity in Hong Kong is such a floating signifier that you don't know what's about to happen?

LEUNG: That, in a way, creates anxiety, but it also makes one more fluid, more flexible in accepting others.

WAH: It is curious, isn't it, that Hong Kong, being a small enclave, an island, hasn't developed a strong sense of a cultural community, as opposed to other "island" communities.

LEUNG: In recent years, because of the 1997 issue, there seems to have developed a stronger sense of identity. But for many years, I guess because Hong Kong is such a site of migration (primarily mainland Chinese coming and then going back, or just stopping briefly on their way through), before 1970 there wasn't really a writing community.

WAH: What happened in 1970?

LEUNG: The late sixties was a period of dramatic change for Hong Kong. The Cultural Revolution began in China. Various ideas and cultural movements from the west were also introduced. Both these forces had a tremendous impact on Hong Kong culture, creating a transformation period in its development. Hong Kong's cultural identity took on many affinities with but also distinguished itself from both China and the west. What happened in 1967 was important. There were riots because the Star Ferry wanted to raise the rate five cents and the protests became symbolic of the general discontent of the people. There was a great gap between the few very wealthy and the multitudes of poor.

WAH: Was this class consciousness influenced by what was going on in mainland China?

LEUNG: Yes, in a certain manner. But it started off in the most spontaneous way—local student dissatisfaction, a strike at a factory, and so forth. These things came together in a spontaneous protest against the living conditions in Hong Kong. So the leftists in Hong Kong, very much aware of what was going on in mainland China, wanted to use the occasion to overthrow the Hong Kong government. So it turned into organized violence conducted by the leftists in Hong Kong.

WAH: Was it anti-western?

LEUNG: It was mostly anti-British. Now, the general public had mixed feelings. On the one hand they were not satisfied with their lives and on the other hand they didn't identify with what was going on in mainland China at that point. They were less idealistic than French intellectuals like Sartre, who looked at Chinese communism as a utopian thing. Many Hong Kong people, however, didn't really identify with Hong Kong leftists or with mainland practices. When the leftists murdered an outspoken radio dj a lot of people in Hong Kong were turned against extreme leftist ideology and practices. Subsequently, one of the effects of the riots was that during the seventies, in response to this rejection of British colonialism and Chinese communism, the Hong Kong government suddenly tried to do a lot of things—improve living conditions, create better access to education, social welfare, housing, and so forth. An awareness of Hong Kong as different from the mainland and different from Britain emerged from this political context. In cinema and literature we can look at the seventies as a kind of formation period. So maybe the contemporary identity of Hong Kong, though we can't say this too clearly, was formed after 1967.

WAH: Was there a "cultural community" arising out of the seventies?

LEUNG: We could say so. People born in Hong Kong after 1949 were grown up and started doing things, writing, doing radio or TV documentary, forming bands, and writing popular songs. Prior to that, literature was primarily nostalgic memories of the mainland denigrating the present in comparison to the past. So it was our generation of the seventies that was the first to write about this city, about its formation and development.

WAH: Let's step back a bit to your own situation, paradoxically caught in your resistance to English and to the purity of Chinese. How has this resistance, embedded now in your own poetics, actualized itself in your work?

LEUNG: Well, we're talking about these things from a 1996 perspective, but at that time, in my struggles, I was not as clear as I am now. In recent years I've become more interested in discerning my own positions in relation to Hong Kong and consequently I've started to write more criticism. I'm not representative, perhaps, but I want to articulate a situation about which not that many people are aware.

When I started in the late sixties, I didn't know how to write about the city. As a young kid I liked to walk around the streets. I'm not a football player or anything like that, so I read a lot. My parents came from the mainland and brought with them a respect for new literature, so I read a lot of modern Chinese literature and foreign literature in translation, but I had not read anything about Hong Kong. Even when I studied Chinese texts in elementary and secondary school, they were always about Nanjing and Beijing, other places. I was not satisfied with that. Even today we rarely use texts written about Hong Kong. It was always these other places that were more important. So when I started writing I wanted to write about my situation, and it was those discrepancies and differences which became the problems I was faced with.

One of the solutions to my dilemma was translation. I had studied foreign literature but what was taught was the early literature, the Victorians or the Romantic poets. I wasn't satisfied with that. As well, I wanted something more interesting so I went to the library to read other things. For example, at Star Ferries, they have a newspaper stall where they sometimes get foreign magazines and sometimes there were these underground American magazines circulating: *The Village Voice*, *Evergreen Review*, *Avant Garde*. It was a good discovery for me in the late sixties. And I found some small books of poems published by City Lights—Philip Lamantia, Allen Ginsberg, etc. I guess I was the only one at that time who was interested in those things. And as a kind of training, I translated some of those poems. Later, I translated Gary Snyder, Gregory Corso, and so on.

Actually, I edited some translations of this poetry and it was published in Taiwan in 1971. So I started as a poet as well as a translator. And when I introduced my translations, I would use the occasion to announce a manifesto of some sort, to argue for a new poetics. Through these translations I was able to promote conversational language, daily language, and subject matters. I was able to say, "Now you see there are people who write about everyday things and not about Eternity," and such things. So I started off by seeing solutions from other cultures, and that helped me, in a way, critique my own cultural community. I was able to import secretly something new from the "outside" to justify my experiments. I don't think there were other people reading books and magazines like that on the mainland or in Taiwan at that time. But I did publish some of my translations because they were more lenient on checking translations, especially since it was poetry. So the underground writing I was interested in at an early age seemed to open up new possibilities, a less arty kind of expression.

I was more interested in common people and daily objects, the kinds of things a person growing up in the city could relate to, rather than high-sounding hollow and flowery language. I think I was the only one who subscribed to *Evergreen Review*. It was crazy. I even subscribed to *The Village Voice*. So of course I was then criticized as being too Westernized.

WAH: I experienced a very parallel situation. In Vancouver, in the early sixties, we also felt we were ignored by the centre, Toronto. Our magazine, *Tish*, in fact, started partly because of a comment by someone down east that their alignment was more north-south, to New York. Well we thought, screw you, that's how we feel too. We're more interested in what's going on in San Francisco. So we've had very similar experiences. *City Lights, The New American Poetry 1945–60, Evergreen Review.*

LEUNG: But I was really lonely at the time. I was the only one. But since I did a lot of translation there were more people who were interested in that, eventually.

WAH: But let's get back to the present situation, to these waters of economics that are really at the base of these movements.

LEUNG: Well, those strategies that I've talked about were actually about my poems in the seventies, early eighties. After that I did other things. As to the present situation, I should point to my poems in this collection (*City at the End of Time*, trans. by Gordon Osing) from the early eighties which has a section called "Images of Hong Kong." And from the late eighties I have another series of poems about Hong Kong, again, but this time I was more aware of the visual representation. There were more and more books of pictures about Hong Kong, all kinds of representations of Hong Kong.

Of course, one of the forms in which Hong Kong is represented is the world of commerce, doing business. Living in Hong Kong, writing about Hong Kong, it is easy to fall into that kind of trap. On the one hand, you can avoid that kind of world (the world of objects, commercial objects), not write about it, and think that Hong Kong is a very cultural place. I don't want to take that procedure. I want to acknowledge the world of objects and commerce and to face it. But, on the other hand, there could be another trap, that is you can easily glorify it: we are doing business, we are doing it very well, we can conquer China. That would be another deception I don't want to fall into.

In my latest poems I am trying to address what I was talking about earlier, these object poems. In the classical Chinese mode, it is usually about bamboo or about flowers as representative of characteristics of a person, virtue, morality, and so on. I stole from that kind of poetry and tried to make some use of it for myself in the present situation. We are living in this world of commodities, things. How are we going to deal with that? So, to answer you, I try to make use of this formal poetry, this poetry about objects, to respond to the present situation. But I am also looking for different ways in the use of language. I do not have one method for solving these problems but I'm aware of the world I live in. My poems are not actually representing things but addressing contemporary issues, and in the process I am conscious of my language and trying to do something about it.

WAH: One of the terms, at least in the west, that already seems to have descended on Hong Kong is the word "organization." How would such a thinking impact on your writing? I mean you're going to be "organized" by something else, yet again!

LEUNG: I'm trying to resist the overall schematic sense of things. When we talk about the grand narratives of the British, of the mainland Chinese, of the businessmen, there are so many kinds of stereotypical idioms for Hong Kong, schemes for Hong Kong, so it's very easy when you are using language to be tempted to let those narratives organize your own poem. Also, there's the language of advertising; when I write about objects I could very well use the sweet language of advertising to write about objects, which could make very cute object poems for sale. I don't want to be organized by that kind of principle.

WAH: One of the big organizers, of course, is the discourse of "nation." How is that coming up in your writing?

LEUNG: Okay, this comes to the second thing I want to tell you. The first one is about business, the world of commerce. Then the second thing is nationalism, the nation. Political celebration is not unlike advertising. They use the same language. At this moment my series of poems about the museum pieces is my answer to that type of nationalism.

WAH: That is, to go back.

LEUNG: No, it's not that simple. I started that series of poems, the museum pieces, at the end of 1995. At that particular moment, nationalism was (and it is even now) a very paradoxical thing in Hong Kong. In 1995, when I started writing that series of poems, there were long lines of people queuing up to get their British passports. So there was this general feeling of not wanting to be Chinese, of wanting to be a British subject. But at the same time, in the field of popular culture, in television, there was a revival of interest in Chinese culture. There are many classical Chinese stories being turned into various popular TV series, like *The Story of the Three Kingdoms*. Even Confucius' life was made into a popular TV drama. Suddenly, symbols of Chinese nationalism are popular, the in-thing in Hong Kong. And in the discussion of political issues in the newspapers, we sense a lot of national sentiments again. Now that is really paradoxical. The same group of people trying to get their British passports are uncritically accepting a Chinese nationalism. So currently there are people emigrating while at the same time saying that, no matter what, we are Chinese, we are one family, we have to stick together. Nationalism is coming back as a form of solution to all kinds of social problems. There are more and more people talking about going back to classical Chinese culture as if you will find, underneath Hong Kong identity, pure and original Chinese national characteristics. I don't believe in that; there are problems with that kind of thinking. So my museum pieces are actually a series of dialogues with classical Chinese cultural objects as a kind of re-examination of Chinese culture through these artifacts from various dynasties.

WAH: So your "Museum" series is problematizing the so-called "purity" of the origins of Chinese culture?

Leung: Yes. And I would like to see Chinese culture as more complicated and diversified. Whenever people talk about Chinese culture and nationalism, they tend to simplify everything. They want everybody to try to stick together and resist the outside. So these pieces try to problematize such ideas, looking at cultures as interacting, evolving, and always having to face new challenges.

china journal

960813 1:45 PM VANCOUVER AIRPORT

Bored – ing!

"Dead time" critiques the oil engineer who works in Libya thirty-five on thirty-five off of flying. Now, a couple of days later at Gate D93, flight delayed an hour for Beijing, I pick up or mumble around that notion of "dead" time and with *Dead Man* movie resonating in background along with "what if dying means you are dead already?"

The flow back into China and black hair. That visage, not of me but of that little blood part of me—does it matter which part—quarter, quantity. The customs agent, a young Vancouver Chinese-Canadian guy looks up after checking my ID: "I was expecting someone Chinese, but you shouldn't assume," he reminds himself when he sees me. I wonder what it would be like without such minor complications (reminders) of identity, expectations, appearance. Do George Bowering and Vic Coleman ever wonder about themselves in that way, ever test or question their skin or names against a norm of race?

Aiming at:

Nanjing (Originals)	Che Qianzi Zhou Yaping Hong Liu Zhang Ziqing
Suzhou (Originals)	Yi Cun Haung Fan Xian Meng
Shanghai	Liu Manliu Mo Mo Chen Dongdong
Kunming	Hai Nan Yu Jian
Beijing	Xi Chuan Mo Fei Wang Jiaxin Zhou Jingzi
Hong Kong	Leung Ping-Kwan

960814 8 PM Beijing Hotel

I'm met at airport by Chinese Ministry of Culture person, Zhang Min. She gets me to hotel and helps change some money. We have tea in my room, and she explains that Xi Chuan has agreed to interpret and help me meet poets I've mentioned in proposal. After some phone calls she says she can't reach him. He calls after she's gone. His English is fairly good; he suggests we get together in the morning.

Trying to jump the jet lag. Nice room on 11th flr of Beijing hotel, posh. Just went for walk up Wangfujing. I strained to find the familiar; construction, McDonald's, many department stores, rumbling changes since I was here in '81. And cars, cars, cars. But still lots of bicycles. You can buy just about anything. I buy some bottled water, beer, and instant noodles.

960815 9:30 AM

Nice walk this morning from hotel looking for street food breakfast and find it over on Dongsi Beidajie where I have a very greasy bean paste ball (at least recognizable from home) and a kind of rolled pancake filled with rice noodles and vegetables—excellent. I have two of them for five yuan (about $1). I'm silent, no language, so I just point and gesture. Now that the Chinese are used to foreigners there's very little gawking to contend with. In fact, I'm now the one doing most of the gawking. Self-conscious gaze and cameraing the scene.

Waiting for Xi Chuan to show up at my hotel room to yak about possibilities in Beijing—whom to meet, how to handle the city. Questions to ask him about the containment and present construction of Chinese poetic language.

We talk for awhile in the room, drink tea, feel one another out about poetry, until I realize he's a smoker and I suggest we go out for tea or lunch. Very hot and humid as we walk up east side of Wangfujing Dajie looking for place to eat. He finds us a little place, and he orders noodles with egg and I noodles with beef. We talk about Yu Jian and other poets, general sense of poetry in China. He mentions Yu Jian's "Zero Document" (Yu Jian gives me a copy of *File Zero*, a collection of postcard images and poems, later in Kunming), a long poem that he thinks is important but with which he doesn't necessarily agree.

Wonderful walk back to hotel talking about "culture," which he thinks is too split between high and low. We make arrangements for tomorrow when he will take me to his school area—Academy of Arts where he teaches English—out near airport, late afternoon.

Tonight I go back to Dongsi Beidajie. Seems to be a better food street. I find a pretty good restaurant—tofu with cilantro, plate of eggplant, potatoes, green peppers, rice, beer —25 yuan (little over $4)—plus nice young waiter from Harbin who speaks English and is happy to try it out on me. Harbin, northern cuisine. I didn't try the dumplings with ginger. The food's greasy but very tasty.

Leans over and down to his noodles and slurps.

Lift my bowl to my lips, sip.
Brings his face down to the bowl on the table, tilts it slightly, and shovels and slurps the noodles and liquid into his mouth with noise, fullness, fillness.
We eye each other, watch our eating.
Same noodles.

Little beggar boys out with their mothers on the streets at night use the kow-tow jab hello hello money, pick at my arms, legs, step in the way, hey money, money. No. Now here, too.

She's sexy street corner in her tight long white dress and she slithers all over him, no shirt, crew cut, tight tummy, long white cigarette between teeth, they flash themselves out in the crowd as flashy whitenesses, hot and testy Beijing night.

I walk along Chang'an Jie towards Tiananmen and I guess I set up more of a difference than usual, wearing my Dorfman Crusher felt hat. A guy on a bench lets out a really strong smile, almost laugh, so that I smile right back at him but walking away feel bad about doing that, proving back to him my own place of potency, white, now I am white and act it out in the face/smile of this guy who's just noticed difference and let it out, his own, same social place, there, on a bench, the heat and humidity tarmac throughout the city over us, heads testing the difference.

Xi Chuan's poets

Chen Dongdong—Liang Xiaoming—Liu Manliu—Meung Lang—Mo Fei—Mo Mo—Wang Jaixin—Xi Chuan—Xue Di—Yan Li—Yu Jian—Zai Yoming—Zhang Zhen—Zhao Qiong—Zhen Danyi—Zhou Jingzi—Lu Yimin (woman in business)—Wang Ying, Shao Caiyu (Shanghai)

Questions for Xi Chuan:

- Why pseudonym? (Liu Juen is real name)
- What/who would you include in an anthology of contemporary poetry? (list above?)
- Who is important to you in the Chinese language?
- What do you think of Hong Kong and Taiwanese poets?
- Which of Wang Ping's writers (listed in *Rif/T*) are women?
- Are you at all interested in borrowing forms (ghazal, utaniki, etc.) from other cultures?
- Do you adopt older Chinese forms?
- Deconstruction or construction of the holy, the cult-ish, the ideal, re Michelle Yeh.
- Does poetry have anything to do with social change?

Stuff it boy scout
Your militaristic upper lip lisps tourism
The Imperial brick bridge
        over conquered water
Grab it

Be looked at—and I look into space—avoid (contact!) (and

right now I turn to find a young guy looking over my shoulder as I write this).

Breasts usually small—under newer western fashions, tight dresses push out the falsies, cups.

She's riding a bike and wearing lace gloves.

Noon. In sidestreet restaurant w/ Tsingtao beer and trying to order tofu and vegetables. The girl struggles with my English, and I feel guilty for only having that, imposing my lack.

The babies all seem to be boys and spoiled too.

Nice quiet restaurant (but w/ muzac), worth the extra few yuan.

Excellent lunch of vegetables (not too greasy), stir-fried lettuce, tofu w/ scallions, mushrooms, lots of garlic, rice (slightly unpolished).

Outside bicycle stand—she's paid under *yi* yuan.

Come out of the cafe, mushrooming
humid back into the hot day
pavement neutral desert, hawk
into the gutter stray gob rice caught
throat pollution.
Sudden face
in face she's at me arms akimbo
miming no-no and finger scolds
across my eyes, distanted tongues

all her language backing up her book
of tickets old citizen cadre street cop
ten yuan (ok finally understand)
—fined for spitting in Beijing

960817 Saturday Beijing 3:15 pm

Last night went with Xi Chuan and Huaizhou Liu (her boyfriend is Saskatoon poet Tim Lilburn who put me in touch with her and Xi Chuan) out to Xi Chuan's room at the Arts Academy in suburbs, towards airport. Taxi thirty-five yuan each way. Sat around his apartment (one room, porch, bathroom w/ wall shower, small kitchen w/ washing machine, closet where he writes) one wall lined w/ books. He says village is dirty but he plans to use all that dirt in his writing. We talk mostly about my writing—he has questions—(I think I talk too much, I should have the questions). I try to give them a sense of my context as "Chinese-Canadian" writer so I wax a little positionally.

Turns rural dark dark and three of us go out to local restaurant for fish (Huaizhou's fave), chili tofu (apparently Tim Lilburn's fave), chicken and peanut, corn, lily shoots, flat peas, beer. Nice pecky meal—too much; Xi Chuan takes a doggy bag. We hurry a little heading home because Huaizhou has to catch subway in opposite direction. She and I agree to meet at eight Sunday morning for trip out to countryside temple where she grew up.

Talk in taxi on the way back about lack of female poets; Xi

Chuan a little at a loss to take that on. Huaizhou talked earlier about "political correctness." Even she seems prepared to let it be.

All the dirt that fits—

Lost into the back alley of the living—taxi still pushes mind blur of traffic into pothole and bike body—Xi Chuan's beast the minotaur—lost in the dark stairwell—architecting his paradigm of dirt—no crows, finally the cicadas quiet down as the warm evening settles, cardgame on the doorstoop of the hutong, dusk and the dust smoking against old bricks, earth grounds the heart.

Very relaxed morning—tea, noodles, bath, reading stuff Xi Chuan gave me last night. At eleven I start out along Jianguomen Daije to Friendship Store, old touchstone from earlier tourist days. Extremely hot (about thirty-eight C) and humid trip—and tiring. Takes me about an hour. Just about try Pizza Hut but the lineups too much. Baskin-Robbins next door has pizza slices for seven yuan (about $1.50) so that's what I have, a Coke, and then head back, hunting a little for some bottled water along the way. Shower, wash sweaty clothes. Now cooled down after a shower and a cold Beijing beer, waiting for Xi Chuan to come by to take me to meet the Beijing poets.

No. 50 Huang Tingzi Bar is in NW of city and is run by a poet friend of Xi Chuan's, Jian Ning, also a filmmaker (*Chinese Moon, Black Eyes*). Others there are Mo Fei, Shu Cai, and another whose name I didn't catch. Zhou Jingzi couldn't make it but sends along, from himself and Mo Fei, a copy of a Spanish-published antho of contemporary Chinese poetry (*Equivalences*) with both Spanish and English translations.

We sit outside on a patio in extreme (for me, at least) heat. Beer and tea. I drink lots more beer than they do. They have wives and girlfriends there who seem to be at another table. Xi Chuan's girlfriend brings a Brit who's lived in Beijing for three years, so after evening's conversation I get an interesting take from her. She's annoyed by their (particularly Mo Fei's) dismissal of the Taiwan and Hong Kong writers. She thinks Beijingese are becoming too self-confident (and self-centered). Mo Fei is the most vocal of the group.

Conversation starts around translation and they question Shabo Xie's translation of my own stuff that I've handed out to them. We all seem to agree on the problem of transparency, particularly Shu Cai who reads and speaks French and has translated some Riverdy. They praise Xi Chuan's translations of Borges.

Their response to my question about the lack of women writers is a blank. Silence, quizzical side glances.

Heated discussion, briefly, about "language poetry," which they all seem to dislike. So they're critical of Zhang Ziqing's and Yunte Huang's translation and publication of Bernstein,

Sherry, and Lazer. But I'm not sure they understand the poetics of "language poetry"; they have a lot of questions about LP. The posturing by Mo Fei, and less so by the others, re their relationship to the outside, seems a little self-centered—though the connections with Shanghai and Yunan poets appear strong. I think they're reacting to my interest in the Nanjing-Suzhou so-called "language" poets and in the social and the diasporic. I can't get any sense from them about ethnic writers in China.

But it's a good evening and Xi Chuan is a very useful and generous interpreter. His own poetry seems an interesting mix of lyric sensibility (though he's praised for not using "I") and formal innovation. He's also quite well read and thoughtful about writing.

960819 Monday

Yesterday Huaizhou Liu took me out to the temple at Hairhou. She was born there and her parents still spend summers in a peasant's house in the village. Her parents were academics and during the Cultural Revolution were sent out to Hairhou to teach in a small school (a Buddhist temple converted by Red Guards) and be re-educated. The temple has been restored as a tourist attraction and Haizhou and I wandered through it briefly only to discover that her first home had been demolished by the restoration. We sat in the shade under some trees and talked since my stomach felt a little tender and I didn't have a lot of energy. We managed to get a taxi for the hour-long ride for eighty yuan—a bargain—so the trip was quite pleasant. We had a wonderful time in her parent's yard; they basically live outdoors in this heat. Her mother cooked up fresh food from the garden—cornbread, weedy greens and garlic, tofu, cucumber, and tomato. They had black eggs but I didn't try them. She came back into town with us in a rickety but cheap taxi. Quite a good day.

for Huaizhou

mother's green's
garlic

like your father
fist

family bodies sister
skin

inside that egg
100 years

outside distances
lime

fine ash, salt
and straw

Last night drinks and dinner-walk with my Canuck compadres, Roger Lee and Kai Chan (Lee Pui Ming had gone to bed, tired from the long flight).

Finally cooled off a little overnight from two days of intense heat and humidity. Today I meet with Chinese Writers Association people.

4 PM. Just back from meeting with Jin Jianfan, Ye Yanbin, Niu Baoguo, and one other, a critic, all representatives of the Chinese Writers Association (government approved). I received a lecture on the nature of Chinese poetry from Mr. Jin and an explanation from Mr. Ye on why the Misty poets and the Campus poets have not been successful—i.e., their poetry is hard to understand by the general reader. I cringe at the power of construction these people hold. As soon as I could I steered the conversation to the "Association," its response to Taiwan (good from Ye Yanbin) and Hong Kong and other matters such as ethnic minority writers (they have a committee and have created a magazine only for "ethnic" writing) and women (ten per cent of five thousand members, but rising since 1949).

A disheartening meeting with power. I long for the open tongue of Xi Chuan. Tonight we have another official function; dinner with Ministry of Culture people.

960820

This is a stomach pausing.
Way up that street of potholes

on the other side of Behai Park

Madame Politics looped her jail term.

The cure for diarrhea is not food.

Take plenty of liquids

deflect attention to the word

read Urumqui.

Raining and, thankfully, a little cooler today. Huaizhou has kindly set up meeting with Wang Jiaxin for the afternoon. He's a very confident writer and speaks knowingly about international writers. We go to tearoom south of Tiananmen. He talks of context and discourse, reads a little Foucault and Derrida. Uses "soul" a lot. Likes "language poetry" like T. S. Eliot; Ashbery rather than Ginsberg. His wife is doing comp lit PhD in Oregon; she's translated Atwood. Nice guy, a bit of an "internationalist." But he has a good sense about how writing works for him.

960821 Wednesday Beijing

cloisonné fish

in the restaurant

shell fish

for lunch

dao fu

rice w/ cold dish

of cucumber salad

slightly pickled
words silent
beyond the window
bike stand
pay for it

960822 Beijing—Nanjing

After nearly two-hour taxi ride through huge traffic jams to airport, a little anxious going through ticketing and security because of lack of directions, but I just follow the flow and I'm now on Shanghai Airlines Flt. 156. Unsure of what awaits me over next six days until I meet with Zhang Ziqing who I'm counting on to set up meetngs with the "Originals" in Nanjing and Suzhou.

Good airplane lunch of rice, beans, meat, beer.

flying into Nanjing
waiting for the ringing
writing out my naming
fathering the landing
body intestinal ginseng
greening the furnace city
liminal [the black hair
of her armpits, body
lifting
this bell ringing hyphen

weighting
Chinesing ending

THURSDAY NIGHT ABOUT 10

After afternoon and evening of intense discussion w/ Zhang Ziqing, Huang Fan, Zhu Jun, Yi Cun, first at my room at Nanjing University and then at expensive restaurant where the food much better than Beijing (shrimp, chicken, pork, beef, tofu—meat very fatty but tasty and sidedish of soya, as opposed to none in Beijing). Great talkers these guys.

Ziqing does interpreting, but he gets sidetracked into arguments w/ the poets. He's fairly knowledgeable about American poetry and has translated and published, with Yunte Huang, the *Selected Language Poems* of Charles Bernstein, Hank Lazer, and James Sherry. He's central pin in connections w/ the Chinese "language" poets I want to meet with here and in Suzhou.

Huang Fan is a very likable "Original" poet, serious, a little English, worked w/ Jeff Twitchell as a student at Nanjing University.

Zhu Jun is a younger poet, after the Originals, considers himself a pure language poet. No English but very engaged during discussions.

Yi Cun was, apparently, a successful "Misty" (writing under the name Lu Hui); he changed his name when he became an "Original." He feels close to my own sensibility. He's now a businessman, chainsmoking, constant cell-phone in and out of breast pocket.

After dinner we walked back to Ziqing's apartment and argued about Stein, ate watermelon, and sweated out the ninety-degree humidity.

My room at the university is air-conditioned. Sightseeing in the morning with Huang Fan and Yi Cun and then a formal session with a group of writers in the afternoon.

Jade Rabbit
equals moon

Dead Man =
  nv s ble
tr ck

the period
a mirror
for roast potatoes

my name is . . .

Huang Fan
a yellow tree

the bottle
is garbage.

960824 Train to Suzhou

Sitting across from Sam Chin, from Chicago, in China as a consultant for GM. He's going to Suzhou too so he'll help me negotiate the get-off.

Yesterday was quite good. Toured in the morning with Huang Fan and Yi Cun—Sun Yat Sen mausoleum—ancient Ming Wall. Great treat was the Nanjing lunch of eighteen courses—very small dishes of vegetables, meats, soups, eggs, noodles, etc.—each dish distinct—only one dish I couldn't stomach because the smell put me off. Very nice to be with Yi Cun and Huang Fan. Fan's English is enough for minimal conversation.

Afternoon I gave talk for writers' group at a mansion on top of mountain—built for brother-in-law of Sun Yat Sen and Chiang Kai Shek. Shang Ziqing asked me to talk about Canadian poetry rather than complicate talk I had planned on "noise." They all got into arguments during question period—and Zhang would start arguing rather than interpreting. Went until late afternoon and then we walked down the hill for supper—mediocre meal with lots of beer, lively discussion. Back to hotel to arrange meetings in Suzhou with Che Qianzi.

jade rabbit
year of the ox
age, my age
after liberation
June 4 or 64
dynasty and long wall

after 2000 what
cars like rabbits

960825 Sunday Train from Suzhou to Shanghai, 5:50 pm

Wow! What a couple of packed days w/ the Originals (Che Qianzi, Zhou Yaping, and Hong Liu (she's Yaping's wife and Qianzi's sister—first woman poet I've met here).

Both three-shower days and I haven't had one since I left Nanjing. Stayed at Zhou's home—fairly recent modern apartment on eighth floor. Very nice people, generous, a grandmother around to handle their small child. Too hot to sleep—I've been spoiled by air-conditioned hotels.

After they, with interpreter Wang Yiman, picked me up at the train station, we dropped off Sam Chin—he going to visit in-laws in Suzhou—then we went for large lunch w/ beer. Got to know one another and late afternoon went to Zhou's and Hong's place where we got into long talk on poetry, particularly about *Parataxis* and that they hadn't received copies of the publication. Late, around nine, whole family goes for visit to night park and then a very good supper of duck's tongue.

Got to bed about midnight. Much kerfuffle all evening about getting me a train ticket and having me met in Shanghai by one of Zhang Ziqing's students.

Today they made TV interview (Zhou Yaping works for local TV station) with Zhou and Che Qianzi supposedly asking me questions about western poetry but they ended up using the occasion to mostly focus on the Originals, their own work.

Went for lunch with new interpreter, a bit of sightseeing on the canals, and then finally got me on train. Station was complicated but Che Qianzi helped wonderfully (though he has no English). I'm pooped. Try to recoup later.

try tea

green canals of continuity to the edge of my
dream I had a rill over the tidal plain my plan
was entrepreneurial but I only remember feel-
ing pure, behind the wall of ocean were her legs
outstretched and cooling
or rice!

960827 Tuesday Shanghai Park Hotel 11:15 am

Rather trashed yesterday and still quite tired today. The travel work has overtaken me so I've decided not to contact Chen Dongdong here but rest for a couple of days before flying to Kunming. Our group (Roger Lee, Kai Chan, Lee Pui Ming, and myself) is touching base here before we all move off in separate directions again).

I'll see a little of Shanghai today after lunch with Pui Ming. The heat and humidity takes its toll. I'm also a little tired of the inclination of the Chinese writers to negotiate a representation in the "west." My TV interview in Suzhou, for example, was mostly about the Original poets and how important

I thought they were to the North American audience.

> *"Stones come from the world" display jade value sitting there worthless as the silk on the 5th floor style now lagged out sleepy salespeople lined up with no war left but money now flowing past the shiny dark mahogany treasures of history become trinkets or grids for museum mind who cares antique CL   THING AND CO. the media not just message messed but the only food available to the beggars and urchins pinching arm insistent on the touch of stone in this filthy world.*

Yesterday met with culture ministry guy in morning to get flight to Kunming lined up (6:30 tomorrow morning). Then went with Roger and Kai to new Museum of Art—gorgeous building and fine display of bronzes and porcelain. Spent afternoon walking and looking at commercialization of this city. Last night went for dinner with Roger, Kai, and Pui Ming to an old restaurant in Bund district. Afterwards we walked along the new Bund promenade by the Yangtse—very leisurely. Roger and I walked back to hotel along Nanjing Road, about an hour through late-night, low-lit street.

> *Nanjing Road is the main thoroughfare past my hotel and's needed on this page as a geographi-*

cal plot line for reading through the quickening
and too early summer darkness of Shanghai
though the rhythm in that change of light does
not quite reach the margins here and neither
that rumbling clothes dryer of humid air outside
nor the air-conditioning of the room can hold
these words cooled in the gutter of the note-
book as I close it nor out there in the gutters of
the night now turning to food and other bodies.

960828 Wednesday

Plane from Shanghai to Kunming—hope to meet Hai Nan and Yu Jian and see a city that is a little different from the highly commercial eastern cities—but probably not.

Flying into Kunming can only mean.

Questions:

- The "high brow" avant-garde?
- Search for an international master poet?
- What is this cultural negotiation w/ the west?
- Minorities (Kunming is noted for its minorities).
- Women (Hai Nan) finally?
- What is editorial window of *Da Jia* (Great Master) magazine?
- Yu Jian—How has *60 Poems* been received, reviewed, translated?
- How interested are you in translation?

• What aspects of composition are important to you?
• Do you, like some of the Beijing poets, use formal innovation to distance social and political dogma?
• Xi Chuan says he's paid 2,000 yuan for publishing in *Da Jia*. Is that reasonable payment?

YUAN

YOU ON

YOU WON

YOU OWE ONE

YOU AN' ME

YOU END!

Picked up at airport by Gu Qun from Foreign Affairs Division, Cultural Department of Yunnan Province. We take taxi to nice hotel and I have afternoon on my own. He says check out Yunnan Nationalitie Village. He writes Chinese characters in my journal which I then show to taxi driver: "I want to go Southwest Commercial Building."

Fifty yuan taxi out to Minorities Village, moderately interesting outdoor replication on the outskirts of the city. I managed to get a bus back into the city for two yuan and got off in what I thought was roughly the centre and started walking. Turned out I was within walking distance of Kunming Hotel.

960829 Thursday Kunming

This morning I had a meeting with Yu Jian and Hai Nan that

was pretty frustrating. The government interpreter, Gu Qun, was not, I could tell, doing a very satisfactory job. So I asked if I could record our session, with the notion that I could have their answers translated by someone back home. But, though the two writers agreed to the taping, indeed, encouraged it, Mr. Gu forbade it. Yu Jian, particularly, showed consternation. Thus the questions and answers were very simplistic. Every time I mentioned the name of a writer I had met earlier on my trip, Mr. Gu questioned the writers and then wrote in a notebook. I could see Yu Jian was hesitant to engage through Mr. Gu. Nonetheless, I had confirmed most of the impressions from others in Beijing about Yu Jian's attitudes.

Hai Nan is also a novelist and, I sense, more traditional, though, from looking at her photo-pose in her books, she seems to be playing into a kind of soft and erotic Miss Misty representation (very Hong Kong commercial?). They both gave me books so I hope to get a clearer sense when I get home and have my colleague Shaobo Xie look at them.

The four of us plus Mr. Lee, the chief editor of *Da Jia,* went for a pretty nice lunch where I tasted roasted baby silkworms. Lots of chili in the food and a great emphasis put on the medicinal value of some of the soups and condiments (since Yunnan province is known for its great variety of plants). I slipped Yu Jian my hotel information in the hopes he'll engage some friend of his who can speak English and contact me for further conversation.

960831 Saturday

Leaving Kunming this morning for Hong Kong. Pretty good visit as it turned out. Yu Jian did call me so we had another chance to meet. His interpreter, Yang Jinqing, a young man who teaches English at Yunnan University, has pretty good language skills so we were able to have more intense and valuable dialogue than the day before. We went to Yu Jian's apartment in the north end of the city and a Hani (ethnic minority) poet, Guo Bu, joined us. We were able to talk specifically about Yu's resistance to international elitism, his sense of what's important in poetry (ordinary, actual language), and, usefully, we got into his "fragmentation" (which, it turns out, is really breath phrasing). Conversation also turned to Guo Bu and senses of ethnic marginalization. He's fairly happy w/ his lot, feels honoured by being recognized by Provincial Writers' Association. He writes in Hani and then translates himself into Chinese.

We talked for a couple of hours and then went for an interesting dinner at a busy, local on-the-street (literally) restaurant. Bacon, duck rind, fried tofu, stewed tofu, something that looks like ham, corn soup, noodle-tomato soup, egg rolls, and a few other things, rice last. Beer and tea. Pretty decent meal, though I'm getting tired of meat.

eating Kunming
meaning missing
letters missing

you absence makes
all day inging
ache song de
note signing
city fitting

Kunming has been a fairly easy city. Good walks within a few miles of hotel for photos and shopping for gifts. One of four days rain. Otherwise moderate summer weather (nice to be away from the steampots of the coast). But pollution and traffic a problem here as elsewhere.

Strangle Six

fragment actually is such a city that might shake the lingo up and in the simulacrum of an earlier Vancouver kick past some door on Hastings as if it were the On Lok on a Sunday afternoon so we might be right during those wet, grey seasons some European intermezzo on Robson silencing Cambodia and John A.'s map with its considerable anguish for the approaching labyrinth our poor daughters are immediate frontiers of the subject I'm thinking of who would never scoff a feast or possibly the goal isn't worth it diction and dictation moments usually bring new weather

When thinking manoeuvres the horizon by fragment rather than whole, by difference rather than by synthesis, we escape the prison of intention and denouement, of the assumed safety of settlement. This is a moment of friction, in and out of language that ponders the "door" as a threshold and a site of passage. How those European maps have muzzled the world, how they cannot disperse the horrors of the new internationalism, how "world," in fact, seems no longer possible. The new subject in transformation is not the idealized free-ranging nomad but a twice-shy equivocal guest, just as hungry as always, who doesn't kick but simply pushes gently through that door to almost silently place an order, as wary of mixed grill as of tacos.

Class. Where you are is who you are. The city is continuously contaminated by upstarts from the gravel pits of the interior and by Asians. Identity gets tweaked into a seam that offers other selves and the diverse is suddenly no longer at the edges but downtown. Fungus turns to mould, *voila*!

Writing would have a lot to do with "place," the spiritual and spatial localities of the writer. I see things from where I am, my view point, and I measure and imagine a ~~world~~ from there. Who I am. Am I? Oaxaca, Vancouver, the Kootenay River a thousand years ago or today, my father's father's birthplace, become "local" to me and compound to make up a picture of a ~~world~~ I am native of. Writing sometimes remembers this image, and sometimes it has to make it up. Malcolm Lowry thought of himself as "a great explorer who has discovered some extraordinary land . . . but the name of the land is hell . . . It is not Mexico of course but in the heart" (42). Writers are wonderers. And wanderers. The American poet Ed Dorn reminds us that the stranger in town is interesting because he at least knows where he has come from and where he is going. Writing is sometimes useful that way, not so much with news of the ~~world~~ out there but as some measure that there is at least something out there.

But out there is only meaningful in its correspondence to (an arduously and palpably constructed) in here. I've lived in the "interior" of British Columbia and such a qualification affects my particular sense of what the ~~world~~ (out there) looks like. We go "down" to the coast, which is the exterior, the outside, the city. The spaces between here and there are part of a vast similarity. The towns become predictable (thus memorably comfortable) in their activities and appearances. Castlegar and Prince George, though specifically themselves, share certain aspects of distance, colour, and taste. One feels at home nearly anywhere there are rivers, pulp mills, trucks, the mysterious gravel roads further inward, and similar "local" inhabitants. Down and out there the exterior becomes more. Vancouver leads to other cities and countries. But all of it, out there, is measured from in here. In the particularity of a place the writer finds revealed the correspondences of a whole ~~world~~. And then holes in that wor()d.

When I was eight my aunty Lil took me to a hockey game between the Nelson Maple Leafs and the Trail Smoke Eaters and on the way to the game she turned around to me holding her just-lit lipsticked cigarette between her long painted fingernails and after blowing a cloud of smoke up to the ceiling of the car said If you want to be a Smoke Eater when you grow up don't ever let me catch you smoking.

A few years before I was eight my uncle showed me the German Luger he'd taken from a prisoner both the material and its language then severed from potential into legend.

When I was eight we had a black 1940 Ford two-door coupe with whitewalls and a radio.

About a month after my eighth birthday some big kid tried to beat up Ernie in the middle of the road on Third avenue but I punched him in the chin then he grabbed me and we landed on the hard snow of the road and rolled around until Ernie shouted watch out here comes the bus up the hill.

In April when I was eight my brush with greatness was that Frenchy D'Amour became famous for winning the Briar Curling championship and one Sunday after the victory parade downtown my dad had a drink of whiskey with him in their house next door and from our porch I could see them through the kitchen window.

When I was eight and a half we drove to Fruitvale to get strawberries so that must be why they have always been different.

In the summer of 1947 we parked under a big cottonwood by the river and roasted wieners and drank lemonade then my mom cleaned up the food put it in the truck of the car while my dad took his shoes off stretched out on a blanket on the grass and fell asleep while we looked for fish in the water and threw rocks.

After the war the universal became part of my identity as if I was penetrated by a constitutive lack though who would have wanted to be different certainly not the chinese or even the Italians up the Gulch.

When he was eight he nearly drowned because he slipped on the rocks into the Columbia River but then his dad grabbed him by his underpants and it's worth mentioning how "just in time" was inscribed onto the surface of his body.

I felt sure when I was eight others were six, five, babies, older cousins and so on but I didn't know I was involved in these temporal paradoxes and that I had to lose that perspective in order to account for my own becoming since I was eight and I was being me and that was the same later when I was nine being who I always was.

Just before I was eight I got a hockey stick for Christmas we measured it up to my nose cut it and burnt my name into it with the wood-burning set then taped a black knob on the butt.

That year I would walk downtown over the bridge and drag a stick along a metal railing past houses under maple trees and apartment buildings overlooking the river past the high school the music store the Savoy Hotel and across the street from the bus depot into the Elite where I'd have brown gravy on bread.

When I was eight I could skate on the ice my dad made in the back yard of our house across the street from the river under the grey sky of the smelter up on the hill breathing the skiff of snow Ernie'd sweep early on the shape of the thread between person and object self-amplified generously and unconditionally into brothers of the neighbourhood.

When I was eight mom was thirty-one and when she was twenty-one I was plus zero but I didn't know where any of her came from except Saskatchewan and after supper there'd be crime doesn't *pay* Dick Tracy or she'd read her Book-of-the-month Pearl Buck and I thought what a strange Chinese name.

When I was eight who would have thought that the sheer material factualness of my body would be borrowed to lend the world I was being constructed inside of the aura of "realness" and "certainty" but then who was organizing their thinking around the disruption of *differences* certainly not famous people far away like Mackenzie King or Just Mary.

When I was eight Mickey got hit by a car and in the morning Ernie and I walked to the next block and lifted his cold *stiff* body into a wagon and took him home crying.

When he was eight he practiced how to *kiss* with his cousin Lily at his birthday party and Ernie's dog Mickey ate Ernie's ice cream.

When I was eight the river came over the bridge or could be I was nine and language was already *aging* into a palimpsest that illuminates the power of spring flood.

That spring a baseball came over the *fence* on Sunday afternoon at Butler Ball Park bounced across the road down the bank and into the river.

One day that summer we drove all the way to Nelson and back on gravel roads caught the last *ferry* at Castlegar the Columbia quiet black and flowing down to Trail just like we were but even further.

In a pee-wee pool game I got hit in the eye blood'n stitches
by the big red-headed kid on the Rossland team
who raised the *puck* right at me.

When I was eight my dad took me to the Crown Point after a hockey game and we had potatoes lyonnaise which he said was a *foreign* language but the cook was Chinese.

At eight the social formation of my gender didn't know biology as discourse and it was only within the post-war bourgeois capitalist order that my sexuality emerged as a separate discursive reality and I became interested in *girls*.

In grade two I fell in love with a blonde named Elizabeth who lived in Sunningdale near Sandy Beach where I was lying on my towel on the grass drying off when she and her friends from *that part* of town walked by with ice cream cones.

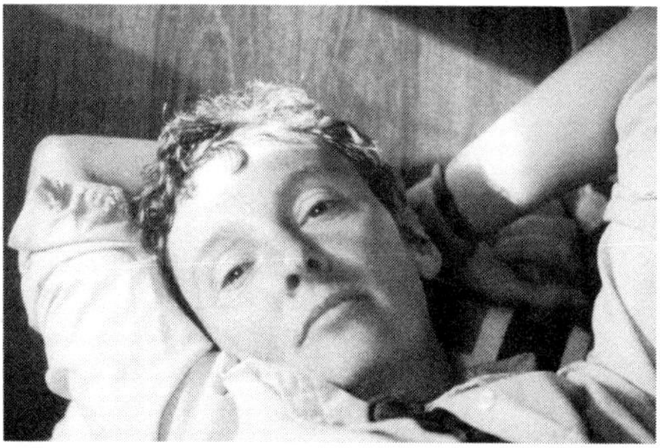

When *you* were eight we lived sixty-four miles apart.

When you were eight you picked up a broken bottle and as you were walking along accidentally gouged your right thigh where you now have a phantom scar that expresses nostalgia for your body's prior *unity* and wholeness just as it etches a kind of "soul" or interiority but could also identify your body should it be found.

When I was eight there was no *question* I would smoke.

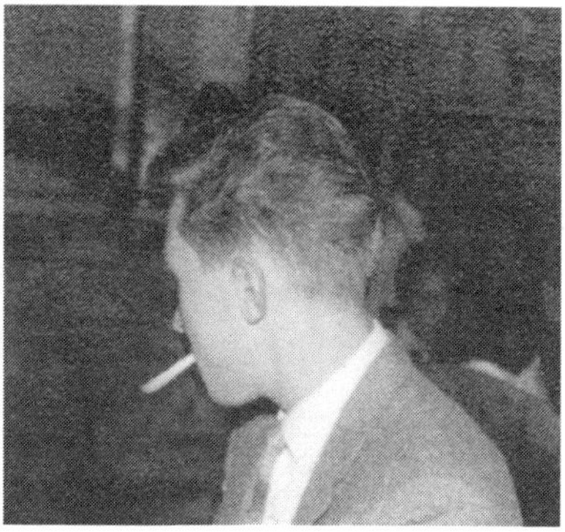

Poetics of the Potent

Nearly every time I type the title of this paper, "The Poetics of the Potent," my left middle-finger flicks out from some secret synaptic desire and types an "e" before the "t" in "Potent." POET-TENT. I enjoy the slip and always correct it. But the almost deliberate embodiment of "poet" with "potent" seems, though obvious, inviting.

I feel invited, in fact, by my friend George Bowering who wrote a short piece called "The Power is There" in which he says he is "told that Fred Wah somewhere said that the poet is a 'technician of the potent'." I'm intrigued by Bowering's discussion of the imputed phrase and by the possibilities to extend my own thinking about poetics. He aligns "technician of the potent" with Jerome Rothenberg's "Technician of the Sacred," Keats' "negative capability," William Carlos Williams' improvisational prose, and Charles Olson's "objectism." He says:

> *Whereas the idea of the sacred is left to human choice, the potent resides in the material and energy particles that might give themselves up to the poem. Not to the poet, but to the poem. The poet, too, should be giving himself up to*

the poem. That is the mystical application of Olson's "objectism." The potent might be apprehended to be in things you can image. I prefer to imagine its place to be in the language itself, in the phonemes we poets must become experts in (101).

The writers I'm interested in have always written from an aesthetic and political position of departure, displacement, decolonization, deterritorialization, and so forth. Space, for most of them, has been the problematics of the blank white page. It has not meant, as it has for some Canadian writers, the desire to substitute for a British or American colonization, the nationalistic self-colonization of John A. MacDonald. The word-world space of poetry and fiction is interested in the unacknowledged world. This "other" space continually generates methods of resistance and intervention. The poetics of the potent is an approach to this discourse.

poti: *lord; power. Skr* patih: *master.* padishah. shah. pasha. Prajapati: *Lord of creation. Gk,* poseidon: *master of earth; god of earthquakes and the sea.* despot: *first master of the house;...* posse: *be able.* potent, potentate, ignopotent,

> impotent, prepotent, omnipotent, plenipotential. ventripotent, *as a glutton.* potential, power, powerful; possible, possibly; possession. *Fr,* puissant. posse comitatus: *power of the county, legal phrase empowering a sheriff to appoint deputies, especially in the American "Wild West," to corral frontier "bad men" (cattle rustlers and horse thieves); the group thus appointed was called a* posse" (*Shipley* 326).

Perhaps it is possible to deflect the gendered value of the term, male potency and power, an underlying "Lordness," to a more useful and equally consequential aspect, that of the implicit ethic hinted at above. We probably should shift to what Bowering says is one of his "favourite theoretical words here: potential" (101). The feminist recognition of empowerment—power *in* rather than power *over*. The writers I'm interested in foregrounding here, for example, would defend their practice against Roland Barthes' attack on poetic fragmentation and particularization of the word (Olson's "objectism") as "a Pandora's box from which fly out all the potentialities of language" (48), "a language," Barthes worries, "in which a violent drive towards autonomy destroys any ethical scope" (50–51). Had he read Québécois poet Nicole Brossard's *Aerial Letter,* where she says that "[i]n writing, I can foil all the laws of nature and I can transgress all rules, including those of grammar" (139), Barthes might have been justly concerned that "the verbal urge here aims at modifying Nature" (51). But Barthes might have recognized the articulation here of a certain poetic ethic, such as I suggest in "A Poetics of Ethnicity" where I try to show that "[t]o write (or live) ethnically is also to write (or live) ethically, in pursuit of right value, right place, (and) otherness" (58). The posture of "otherness" that Brossard assumes is so frequently misinterpreted, as with Barthes. A more acute alignment for an ethical otherness might be Novalis' sense of an antithetical crossing over, mutuality and complementarity.

> *Nature will be moral—if it, through genuine love of art—gives itself over to art —does what art wills—: art, if through genuine love of nature—lives for nature and works according to it. Both must do this simultaneously and of their own free choice—for their own sake—and of necessary choice for the sake of the other. They must meet the other in themselves and themselves in the other (28).*

As Giorgio Agamben suggests, language itself is implicated in a tendering of potentiality that claims it as "contingently necessary":

> Language (reason) is that whereby something exists rather (potius, more powerfully) than nothing. Language opens the possibility of not being. But at the same time it also opens a stronger possibility: existence, that something is. What the

> principle properly says, however, is that existence is not an inert fact, that a potius, a power inheres in it. But this is not a potentiality to be that is opposed to a potentiality to not-be (who would decide between these two?); it is a potentiality to not not-be. The contingent is not simply the non-necessary, that which can not-be, but that which, being the thus, being only its mode of being, is capable of the rather, cannot not-be. (Being-thus is not contingent; it is necessarily contingent. Nor is it necessary; it is contingently necessary.) (104–105)

•◆•

In her novel *Picture Theory*, Nicole Brossard wishes to construct a three-dimensional language, a hologram of potential resemblances and memory. For her, this is a bodied and lesbian utopia:

> *the transparency of utopian silk/self (in my universe, Utopia would be a fiction from which would be born the generic body of the thinking woman). I would not have to make another woman be born from a first woman. I would have in mind only* the idea *that she might be the woman through whom everything could happen. In writing it, I would have everything for imagining an abstract woman who would slip into my text, carrying the fiction so far that from afar, this woman participant in words, must be seen coming, virtual to infinity, form-elle in every dimension of understanding,*

> *method, and memory. I would not have to invent her in the fiction. The fiction would be the finishing line of the thought (148–149).*

In other words, the possibility must be written. Writing holds the potent. She says, in *The Aerial Letter:*

> *I know that writing is memory, power of presence, and proposition ... For in writing I become* everything ... *a process of mental construction which enables me to synthesize that which in life—real life—must be portioned out to fiction and to reality. In writing, I can foil all the laws of nature and I can transgress all rules, including those of grammar. I know that to write is to bring oneself into being; it is* like *determining what exists and what does not, it is* like *determining reality (139).*

Or, as Bowering says in "The Power is There":

> *What is potent? Or where is the potency (the potential)? It is in the possible combinations and recombinations of the basic materials of our language. We can perpetrate fusion at room temperature. God made us happen with a few words. We are the enactment of those*

words. We too can speak. As poets we should be careful of what we think we create.

That is to say, the technician should never get the idea that he is the source of the power. He is vouchsafed the privilege of channelling it, from wherever it was proceeding when it came to him, to wherever he can direct it with care (101–102).

That "care" that Bowering recognizes is Novalis' "love."

In an essay entitled "Corps D'Energie/Rituels D'Écriture," Nicole Brossard draws no line between the political, the aesthetic, and the spiritual. What interests Brossard in writing is the "circulation of energy" (7) through the body which is then "filtered by language" (8). For her, this energy is part of a trajectory into ritual. She talks of the rituals, for women, of "trembling, shocks, sliding, breathing" (13):

I am using the metaphor of ritual to describe what seems recurrent to me in the psychological and linguistic gestures that are ours when, as women, feminists or lesbians, we have to confront censure, anger, but also that joyous enthusiasm that overcomes us when we man-

age to identify the inner certitudes that inhabit us (10).

The strategy of the long poem is by now an old attention, yet a continuing one. In an essay on Lionel Kearns' long poem *Convergences*, Lianne Moyes discusses the dynamics of intertextuality Kearns employs in that poem and cites Julia Kristeva on Bakhtin: "Everything means, is understood, as part of a greater whole—there is a constant interaction between meanings, all of which have the *potential* of conditioning others (15–16; emphasis added). Moyes also fingers Foucault's phrase, "the density of discourse," and I find that a useful attention to materialization and energy parallel, perhaps, to what Charles Olson called "intensivity" (*Muthologos* 80). The intensification of layering, like composting, generates a useful heat, indeed nutrition, a means of recuperating the garbage of narrative extension so dominant in the long poem. I also find useful the overlap between Moyes' recognition of the long poem as a lyric genre and my own sense that the prosodic matrix of the short lyric (syllable, line, and cadence) gains the quality of imminence (read potential) in the long poem.

I should reiterate the oscillation of "potential conversation" that Marlatt recognizes in translation between source and target languages (*Tessera* #6). The kind of potential that most interests me vis à vis translation, both in literal translation as well as translation as a compositional strategy, is the position and place of active apprehension between the two languages. (See the poetics of the trans- in "Half-Bred Poetics"). I'm thinking of interposition, of an open-ended transcreational process where the "being in-between" (thus, intervention) suspends, as Benjamin Hollander writing about translation suggests, "the double-edged gaze of incitement and citation" (35).

That sense of potentiality also exists in improvisation (see "Loose Change") and its concomitant subversion of the solidity of expectation, and it exists, too, at the interface of a hyphenated (racialized) poetics (see, again, "Half-Bred Poetics).

•◆•

Bowering locates potency "in the possible combinations and recombinations of the basic materials of our language" (101).

The fist of punctuation, for example.

Claire Phillips suggests that the potency of the period operates within a system of containment and closure sometimes viewed as a violent act within public discourse (46). She notes, for example, in Steve McCaffery's *Evoba*:

THE. (47)

The period can also function as a signal of silent reflection that clings to the referent, as in the title to Ian Hamilton Finlay's magazine:

Poor. Old. Tired. Horse.

Or as the empty shell of a bullet just fired, the bullet just fired, the extensions of possible suffix in the name of John Clarke's magazine:

Intent.

Even the respiratory connection to the comma echoes punctuation's potency. For Gertrude Stein "commas were unnecessary, the sense should be intrinsic and not have to be explained by commas and otherwise commas were only a sign that one should pause and take breath" (Burke 43).

Another significant aspect of a poetics of the potent would be the re-reading and re-writing strategies generated in the ethnic and feminist rejections of assimilation, the bargaining for a position of the potent in the reterritorialization of inherited literary forms and language. Daphne Marlatt's book, *Salvage*, is another fine example of her untiring attention to the nitty-gritty of writing down (as in hunting down) language. The dust-jacket blurb establishes her intentions "RE" poetics right at the start.

> *From Steveston on the Fraser River, to Vancouver's East End Chinatown, to the discovery of the community of women writers drawn together by language, she* re-traces *her steps through time, over space, and across cultures. Part poem, part fiction, part autobiography, the book* re-reads *and* re-envisions *(her) earlier writings in light of her feminist experiences of the late 80s and in doing so salvages them.*

"These are littoral poems, shoreline poems," she says in the foreward to the book.

They began as a project to salvage what I thought of as 'failed' poems. But the entire book attempts to salvage the wreckage of language so freighted with phallocentric values it must be subverted and re-shaped, as Virginia Woolf said of the sentence, for a woman's use (8–9).

The writing is a "righting" R-I-G-H-T. Again, the ethics in such a poetics envisages a politics. One of the sections in the book, a series of poems she calls "Park (your) dream," maps out a polis of paradise and skid-row:

paradise

the movement is backward
back to hyde park
and pan (peter even

> *enclosed*
> *eden, experience*
> *there in the form of a*
> *drunk*

> > *(what does he bring?*
> > *what other*
> > *ways to seem*

free, and so close in to hell
she said, a wraith, a wrath to us

. . .

clarity and a
magnetic tongue, the lyric
transpose

syntax of old alleys, old
passageways of Pairi-daeza

climbing the walls even
to get over it (53–55)

Though the poetics of the potent is full of power, that power does not reside in a position of authority and imposition. Rather, the dynamics shift through a range of play and invention in order to continually posit possibility, unpredictability, negative capability, and, dramatically, necessity. In one of the maze-glyph cartoons of "Scraptures: Lost Sequence," toward the end of *Gifts,* bpNichol expresses a fundamental compulsion addressed to one of the main protagonists of *The Martyrology*, "st reat":

> *oh my eyes are falling below the levels i speak*
> *to you on and i have come here to some sort of*
> *crossing i would understand the better saint*
> *reat were you here to guide me but you are not*

here and taunt me across the impossible distances of my syntax telling me i am without hope of reaching you as tho to try even were an impossibility an impossibility does not exist saint reat no only you are the sometimes impossible dream of my youth of my passing years you are the words that will not flow from me but become lost in the wake of you passing of your passion or my passion for you and are discarded there fall like nothing else into the traps of your metaphors and similes you will not believe me that i see below all the levels . . . oh saint reat i cannot be still but must follow you forever down whatever road you would lead me and i know you will lead me can i but find the language there (n.p.)

And looking for the right language is, essentially, the fuel for *The Martyrology*. "What is necessary in order to understand is a TOTAL ASSAULT" (*Gifts* n.p.), we read on one page of collaged type. The aggression is more a compulsive propulsion, an explosion forth into language (and Life and Death and Memory and Family, anything that might provide a lead to the next move, the next passage/way). What I find engaging in such writing is the spectrum of potentiality, of energy and the attention and openness to intelligence. And I mean by that term the verb, "to intellect," because resident here is the movement of intellection, discovery, choice, and chance. Consequently Nichol's "continuing" poem gathers to itself an accumulation of energy, a substantial mass palpable by its continually moving parts, a book composition that gains the potency and potentiality of a hypertext of reading.

In order to intervent the tyranny of the conventionally published book space, another type of colonized space for writers, Nichol includes five unbound poems which he directs the reader to interleaf at random among the pages of the bound volume. Thus the eye and heart can chance upon one of these free-floating texts and the poignancy of particularity of the words of his dying days hits with atom-like spinal impact:

sacrum

say
the whole thing ends

say
you're frightened
of the whole thing
ending

say
cheese

say n't

n't ready

n't ready to die (n.p.)

Strangle Seven

The shoulders of eating, the sack full of ginger, the Blakean beach, the other word at the end of the word, the curl from kulchur, the grade for the course, the genome in their home, the rap at the door, the spoon full of the rice, the chop for the lick, the tongue in a knot, the circuits of surplus, the milk on the way, the valley behind the valley, the end of the world.

No mass is without something else, something added, other. The one and the many. Taste is a gradation of foreignicity: he comes across some discarded particular with the realization that it isn't in the lexicon of culture surrounding him. These particles of recognition and desire, subalterns and alternatives, are what he uses to intervent and localize those homogeneous aggregates of institution and industry that contain him.

In Jim Jarmusch's movie *Dead Man*, William Blake (played by Johnny Depp) finds himself in Machine, a frontier Dickensian factory town at the end of the line. The frontier is, of course, Hell. There, Blake is wounded, transformed into an outlaw, and acquires his first gun. As this white man and his spiritual native guide, Nobody (played by Gary Farmer), set out on a journey of escape that turns into a rite of passage over to the world of the dead, Nobody tells Blake that the gun will replace his tongue. The movie is a tantalizing rumination on the poet William Blake's visions and prophecies contextualized with the technological destruction of the west by the west.

The final question that Jarmusch coaxes from his film is what happens to the soul in the face of this dynamic channelling of the poet's body into the barrel of a gun. The closing scenes are filmed in a Northwest coast native village. The photography ironically implicates those problematic photographs of North American Indian life by Edward Curtis who, according to A. D. Coleman, "set out specifically and deliberately, to capture the spirit of the Indian lifestyle and invest his photographs with it" (Curtis vi).

Derrick de Kerckhove, in his book *The Skin of Culture*, offers a similar qualification of the first photograph of the Earth: "[I]t expands our perception of our self beyond our own body-image and enlarges our sense of identity. Indeed, from the first moment we see that photograph, we take possession of the Earth and of a new power to invest in it. It is an extension of my eyes" (217). It is me! There I am! We are the same! That's the shape I'm in! This is an investment of identification and identity that commodifies otherness not as excessive and relational but as consumable and narcissistic.

The metaphors of theft, containment, and growth suggest a dangerous technological discourse. Am I really that hungry? How much more can I stomach? The ecologist Paul Hawken warns of the liability from such misinformation: "A herbicide kills because it is a hormone that tells the plant to grow faster than its capacity to absorb nutrients allows. It literally grows itself to death" (8). In our desire for technology to metaphorically and literally extend our bodies, we seem to be courting the toxic information of a global market-based economics. Are we not collapsing those very border coordinates necessary for change and movement, exhausting our imaginations in the business of profit (that frontier town, Machine)?

At the end of Jarmusch's film, William Blake sets forth on the Pacific surf in a death canoe that his Aboriginal guide has prepared for him. Nobody tells him that it is time for him to go and join the real William Blake, to go back where he came from. Thus the film avoids, in this Enkidu/Gilgamesh portrayal, the usual western self-centered appropriation of otherness.

I don't need the simultaneity of a virtual reality; I need a tool, such as poetry, to intervent such collapsible subjectivity, something that is an opposite and dis-centered gesture of comprehension.

> *Improvement makes strait roads; but the crooked roads without Improvement are roads of Genius (Blake, "Proverbs of Hell" 185).*

bp's Last Notebook

1.
soft cover and a loud back
June's VEL (lour-vet-lum) notebook
rending "fin" sk.
brief istorine of time, asking
fact art locate reit cf. Catullus

A gift journal from Tom H. (9 July 1982) begun June 26, 1988 resurfacing three days later as "OH, OH TOM MOT, HO HO" above two H headstones mirroring TOM MOT. But page one is a visual of waves and a fin rolling handwritten "end." Time and notes, catalogues, "sketches," and questioning within the self-dialogue (reflection), reminders, collecting what? Some mind full of detail setting sail on what horizon, the glyph-boat, Sanders' "peace eye" in the background, Catullus questioned, either "median" or "Indian" translations, question, scatter held by order of a clean new page, working to hold what? Cites Hawking: "Just as a computer we must remember things in the order in which entropy increases" (n.p.). Fragments of disorder. Meaning mirrored.

2.

series eliminate typewriter draft

seven plus to power of ten

mirrored tomatoes O O O

July 6/88 Edmonton Kristjana's

Regina address over grained W's

The O's become "OH O RIZON" in Edmonton driving there from Red Deer on July 6. Juggling all the series, drafts, project(ile)s, and arriving in Alberta for Red Deer Writing Workshop and the prairie stretches over a July heat of wheat fields addresses and phone numbers (Dennis and Birk) same-day poem "read, dear" for them. Notebook as a listing device, shopping around on the unlined page for a glyph, a glance so much that the page becomes place, a place to be, in.

3.

grammaring saints tinkering

new radio remembering babel

in "fin" sk. Aug 4 now avec "end"

by seven a pregnant pun

rowing around a b cosmology

The chart. Always generative and extending paralogically to gather up as much of the matter as available, given the speed.

Saints as monograms thus grammology thus geneology. The lexical simply as info but trying to push ST further until the charting becomes a condition of geneological memory games, literally a list of remembering and not remembering. The whitecaps become dotted "i's" and "fin" is *translated* "end." "b" becomes the pregnant pun of earth; notes toward equivalence, syntagmatic thought suffixing via the arrow to row your boat gently down the stream, he says. And titles. Every language "event" gets titled.

4.
instructions re incomplete
now absent plotted equal
new series Aug 8 "nsformation"
eg snow water ice steam tea
plus frog reclining side view

After the "Instuctions re Incomplete H" (another exercise at equivalence) he comes on to a new series titled "nsformation." These are minute, what McCaffery calls "eruptions that testify to a radically different semantic order" ("In Ten$^{t}{}_{s}$ion" 72). Only the "a," for example, of "snowflake" transing into the "a" of "water." The paragrammatic attention moves on through more water, tea, steam ice, solid, liquid, paper, fire. Hand over hand, that's the speed. Even shifts into "Big Haiku" of "frog hog log." Followed by "line, lion, and lyin'."

The day's a large run and the quick movement through these micromorphemes gains a kind of spatiality in the notebook, i.e., less intentional than in the Mart. Some notes "re Group" ("the piece is about transcience, situations as transitional, i.e., living w/ that flux," and the H reclines.

5.
at 11:10 pm "limbp" bio
even moment dances
pieces spin BLAM & poof
quote take this visible
is it "kaplooie"

Standing by his word and writing self gesture to the ever-present body. Serials as moments from a life of moments, numbered but not ordered except gesturally into the immediate future present. Yet crucially informed by autobiographical memory like Fred Astaire and Ginger Rogers. Dovetailing and layering the phonological with the morphological, that is, "SOUND EFFECTS as part of a textual poem." He adds "poof" and then "BLAM" becomes a double track of el-em-en-t-s with "KAPLOOIE" (but here in the journal it's more the intellect and the visual—a kind of biotextual self-evidencing and—referencing he opens to in "MONOGRAM/GENEALOGY/GRAMMOLOGY."

6.

a date of round stones
spiralled problems little lines
and circles amazed elements
transed particles acted
out for the selves right here

August 8 has taken fourteen pages. It was a Monday, in Toronto. The day's run ends with the piece undersigned as "date": 08/08/88, that looks like piles of round stones or stacked cordwood. The day has spiralled through a series of concrete and sound-text "instructions," "nsformations," "autobiographical moments," "problems of the self," and notes "re" compositions, performances, and publications. The eyes circle the page looking for text, sometimes in amazement at the connections as pieces of mind, word, and letter spill further onto the surface of presence, to be there, at that page and line the hand makes and mind considers and observes. The instant becomes a convulsion of language and thinking. The body is so still.

7.

mitts writing strict stone
concrete lyric type knot
of voiceness pawed trace

definition gesture print
over & against some notion

A list of re "hand/writing" (Earle Birney, Gerry Gilbert, Andy Suknaski, Judy Copithorne, Sha(u)nt Basmajian, Steve McCaffery, etc.)—"over and against the Typewriter Poem &/or the strict definition of CONCRETE"—wonders where the hand comes into it, he says, "NOT as lyric voice—TRACE?" and then a very Olsonian "over & against PRINT." And then characterizes this notion of this body part as "gesture." The push is against both print and lyric voice and positing a potential "trace" as imprint. Almost expect him to reiterate Olson's "typos," though the problem could be for bp Olson's alignment of the hand with the force of type hitting surface. Trace also more fitting to bp's sporadic notebook mind since so much of writing's production is outline or partial to what gets limned.

8.
facts a book of "patafysical
tearouts you can make six
exciting syllables out of blue
Look! " . . . life/
a life" male or female

Numbering the facts. Truth in numbers. "Discover what governments have known for years." He's playing by the number. A probable system. That is, one that informs. A system that talks back, remembers ("so simple to use a child of six"): 2nd edition, 5 pleasing colours, 26, Can do it by yourself, Easy to use, Order it Now! This is sequence, all these "ciphers" (try to de-cipher his handwriting) a hoped-for crypto-substitution of a symbolic order; the literally cryptic quality of a life—"male or female" (he says vis à vis voice of the reader in "Ad Sanctos"). In order/to remember.

9.
Edwards Gardens Toronto
August 28, 1988 D.
Marlatt moves molten
moon to use "Negatives 6"
absence friction bleeds

A 5–section poem "for & after Daphne Marlatt." The handwriting sometimes indecipherable (almost Ondaatje-like in horizontally disappearing waves) yet certain words and phrases inked over to stand out in a relief of emphasis or recuperation (maybe two different pens): "moves/to use/ play/ mirage/ molten/ go down/ what was once absence/ her/ lack of/ in or/ the and the/ bleeds/ away turn/ out of sight/ moonlight/ of a sudden/ that this/ personal/ visible, scarcely/ love/ that shines/ wait in/ tension/ go into/ I do." The illegible clearly intentional, at least permissable, as a means of movement. This poem-text resonates with earlier notes on "hand/writing" that talk of "Trace" and "gesture" "over & against the Typewriter Poem &/or strict definition jof concrete—" a kind of lyric cryptograph, a hazing of the lyric.

10.
look out for ritualistic cop-
out warns Steve body
parts lining warning poem
paranoia "pair o'" Roy K's
trees @ David B 843–

That should be "vitalistic," not "ritualistic" (I think I was picking up on a resonance with the previous line, "middle initial art," for what that's worth). I wonder how long he argued with the body as a simulacra of code? The "bp:if" series ("body paranoia: initial fugue"), the floaters of *Gifts*, runs August 30th to September 10. Having a body doesn't struggle with being a body. His fear of the disappearing body framed photographically as itself (his body as the performer) and a textural self saying: "say/cheese . . . say n't/n't ready/ n't ready to die." Could be the absence of the "3000 BC quote" is an intentional one.

Dear Hank,

Your package of reading arrived just as we were packing for our ten-week trip to Thailand and Lao. I brought along some of the photocopied material, and yr piece on Ron Silliman's *The Alphabet* has come up as a useful pivot for my thinking here. That and a book Jeff Derksen suggested, Dean MacCannell's *The Tourist: A New Theory of the Leisure Class*, have provided me with some riprap with which to consider my own "tourism" on this trip.

So this epistolary "field" note, journal, krinopoetic utanikki, has been, for me, usefully addressed, at least portionally, to some of the notions of writing and "compositional" ethnography you locate in your essay on Silliman. I've found it useful, in other words, to use your critique for some leverage of my own experience here in Thailand.

I should say that, coincindentally, I pulled off the web (http://ccat.sas.upenn.edu/xconnect) a part of Silliman's "You" to take along for reading before I'd received your package. (Such printouts made for lighter weight packing and were easily dropped in guest houses for print-hungry tourists). I decided I wanted to take "You" along as an instance of poetic notetaking composition that, cumulatively, gains open observational breadth. In "You," there is the effect of dailyness and place, and that persistent talking to oneself (w/out verbalizing), the "vibrant meaninglessness" encountered in the "kind of silence" we find in a writing that is not "pure design" (quotes in this sentence are from Lazer's title page citation of Silliman's *What*).

I'm attracted to the text of "You" because of the quick movement in "perception" (too Olsonian a term?—perhaps it's more "attention") that, as you say, juxtaposing composition allows. The movement that's interesting in "You" is the same kind of shift you locate throughout *The Alphabet*, both syntactic and attentive, that comes from the juxtaposition of non-serial, non-hierarchical, sentences:

> *The aggression of toddlers or of squirrels. Theory of naming evident when we call a black-capped chickadee a bird that more accurately appears to wear a white mask. I carry a sleeping boy up the stairs and to his bed.*
>
> *The word on the net is that you are in France. A large one-story pomo building on an even larger lot turns out to be a hair salon (land use away from the city). How each McDonald's is most apt to differ from one another lies in whatever special accommodation is made for the play of toddlers. Aware of the dewpoint nearing eighty degrees.*

Irked at Adam's meddling, Hayley set a wedding date with Abe, then later went to the beach with Mateo. After defending Kirk to Scott, Sam stunned Kirk by insisting that they start their honeymoon right away. Meanwhile, Nikkie tried to get Amy to show interest in Nick, and then tried to get Nick to show interest in Susan. Luke explained AIDS *to Lucky.*

On the couch, starting to watch a video (Gerard Depardieu as Cyrano leaps and rants about the stage), I virtually swoon into a deep sleep, to dream of a great wall of candy, sugar-coated drops of licorice, white, pink, black. Simple male transfer protocol. Three kinds of woodpeckers about these trees. Atmosphere is a broth.

Old town graveyard after dark, the grass too high, lit only by lights from the nearby church parking lot. A bowl of blueberry frozen yogurt. Large sore on the roof of my mouth. The sweltering sky.

Hourglass frozen against the screen. First inverted whistle of a cardinal in the poplar. T3 trunk line upgrade rollout—scan that! Differentiate in a boy's mind gravity from mag-

netism from simple suction. Small girl skating down the steepest of hills.

An icon for poetry (winged hearse). Woodpecker walks up the trunk of tree. Light mottled on the large leaf. Squirrel growls (from "You").

As you say, "Silliman writes from a shifting perspective. Often his view is what I think of as a rather neutral camera eye, witnessing and recording 'how lives weave past'" (73). Of course, I'm using a camera here. Trying to figure out how to use it and still negotiate what you call "the polarities of domination and equality" (69) that the usual people-picture taking doesn't. But, perhaps because of the technology, no matter how neutral (or haphazard) I try to be, I realize the camera needs to be hierarchically "set up" before I take the picture. So I'm more noticing my own implication in this construct than solving the "compositional" problem. But your analysis of Silliman's structural method as being "without a hierarchical mode of organization" (69) seems as problematic vis-à-vis homogeneity as, say, Olson's "There are no hierarchies, no infinite, no such many as mass, there are only / eyes in all heads, / to be looked out of" (*Maximus* 33). That is, the opticality, of either taking the picture or recording "how lives weave past" is not a neutral position. Having a camera or a poem is both a privileged and priveleging situation.

For example, at the top of the hierarchy (compositional anyway) is "no hierarchy." It comes around. You cite from Silliman's *What*:

It is not that
there is no narrative
here (each sentence
is a narrative,
each line moves)
but that there is
no hierarchy
of narratives (not even
the story of the
poem), no sentence
to which the others
(all the others) defer
and are ranked
(the map is not
built about the city) (Lazer 70)

Ron's sense of a map not being hierarchical seems useful as a position from which to write, particularly if it undercuts the virtual stability a map usually implies. But just as the ethnographer's notes get configured into continuous narrative, and take their place in our ongoing ideological constructions, so too does Ron's observation become configured in its own cachet of "poem" (advertised through its own shapeliness as such).

My daily writing is confronted by the limitation of mapping, what isn't mappable with my little notes and poems. I'm not that comfortable with the linguistic commodity of tourism (as far as I can tell, most people aren't); but I need something in the writing that operates as, you suggest, Silliman's *The Alphabet* does, that is, by confronting the same problems as ethnographic writing: "[H]ow to represent a culture *while participating in that* culture; how to offer insights into that culture without falling prey to a falsely totalizing perspective; and, at the other extreme, what it might mean to adhere to a seemingly democratic equality of perspective" (Lazer 69).

I think you're fundamentally right about the dynamics of Ron's compositional method, and its usefulness in facing the ethnographer/tourist dilemma of complicity; at the same time, there seems no way out of the implied preponderant influence of the sentence (and the poem) over any present map or observation. I think what I've always resisted about Ron's call to the "new" sentence is that it is still the *sentence* that is posited as an hierarchic morphemic value. I understand Ron's description (and his essay on "The New Sentence" is immensely useful), but the focus on the "sentence level" of language provokes resistance in me as one of those culturally inherited, grammatically dominant concepts that somehow remain in control of our thinking.

Yet I'm not that content either with what my own practice has used in the face of syntactic "rightness" (growing up with definitions of the sentence, complete thought, right!), what I call the "submersible sentence," a run on/run over prose syntax that attempts to deflect the sentence's closures, containments, and, for speech-based writers, cadences. Ron hints at this level as the last of his list of "qualities of the new sentence":

> *The limiting of syllogistic movement keeps the*

> *reader's attention at or very close to the level of language, that is, most often at the sentence level or below (91).*

Why must the sentence be "above" what is "below"? Submersion, not subordination (choice, not privilege).

Iain Chambers qualifies the sentence as a point in the migrant landscape beyond which writing can travel:

> *The point of the author, the point of arrival, becomes the point of departure, and the boundary of the sentence is breached by the surplus of language. In this manner writing can become a travelogue, a constant journeying across the threshold between event and narration, between authority and dispersal, between repression and representation, between the powerless and power, between the anonymous pre-text and accredited textual inscription. It is a journey that finally comes to circulate and take up temporary residence in that disputed border country in which the official account dissolves into the historical infinite of indigenous narration. Here, not only is the particular authority of the sanctioned description questioned, and the empirical claims of reality sub-*

> *ject to scepticism, but the very status of the telling, of language and text, is invested by doubt and dislocation (11).*

The implications are formal. Beyond the sentence's border lies the prose poem.

> *Today, Tuesday Feb 2 Khao Lak hot and sunny:*
>
> *German—maybe Swede then my Honda's beauty if UV skin deep in the climate machine's dream down at 125 cc a piece of rebar w/ two loops welded near the top the beach umbrella bobs the word "boat" w/ its long-tailed diesel want one and I want it on Kootenay Lake could pick up one of those "Ethno G" Casios across the table she says are you Chinese or Japanese? My story just won't end.*

Parasentence. Some measure, the paragraph. At what level the "line," then?

> *Tuesday Jan 12 Samui +30*
>
> The Beach *Leonard di*
> *something boy film*
> *as children do, grains*
> *that sandpaper feet bottom*

sun circles shadow
as a series of strategies
for skin not clear
about goodness
walked down sentenceless
to the end and back
plastic and shell struggle
rope debris what if
this beach is the hospital
footprint, toes sink
bound the child's capacity
to rust.

Yet how the final period signs what precedes it as "sentence."

Having said that, I'm also very attracted, compositionally, to what the "new" sentence can do in a dynamic of juxtaposition. I like your sense of how, in *The Alphabet*, Silliman neutralizes the sentence's function as rhetorical narrative. Yet one of the aspects I'm attracted to in "You" is how the visible paragraph (as a measure of quantity) clears the poem for phrase and fragment.

> *On the couch, starting to watch a video (Gerard Depardieu as Cyrano leaps and rants about the stage), I virtually swoon into a deep sleep, to dream of a great wall of candy, sugar-coated drops of licorice, white, pink, black.*

Simple male transfer protocol. Three kinds of woodpeckers about these trees. Atmosphere is broth. ("You" XXX)

Narrative not so much vitiated as opened up, let loose without, as you say, "falling prey to a falsely totalizing perspective" (69).

The aspect of "the immense accumulation of culturally specific observations in *The Alphabet*" (70) that you point to, as one result of a juxtapositional process, is potent. MacCannell talks about "an immense accumulation of reflexive experiences which synthesize fiction and reality into a vast symbolism . . . " (23).

990116—Samui

I'm trying to read the "beach bungalow" as a symbol, in Dean MacCannell's terms, not as a symbol "of" but as, perhaps he might agree, a symbol "for" an accumulative experience. We've come here "for" a little R&R, an emptying out, the "negative transparency," to use Bhabha's identification of "the cultural . . . as an articulation of displacement and dislocation" (175) that might reveal an "other," at least something further. I can see where this might go here, leading a little too comfortably, into the discourse of difference. Look at the language we are given.

> *Locate the "beach bungalow" in its lexical production, the brochure: "what ... must have been like 20 years ago"; "uncrowded"; "great food ... cheap rates ... remote ... pretty ... and peaceful"; "overdeveloped"; "crowds"; "accessible (only by boat)"; "basic ... great character"; "old city gates"; "renovated"; "real brewed coffee"; etc. The values expressed by such a language (authenticity, space, economy, quiet, utility, accessibility, familiarity) are all-too familiar extensions of an historical and socially constructed sensibility.*

I feel desultory in my desire to resist coordinating such a "*salvage* function" that James Clifford notes about ethnography (Lazer 70), even through an intentionally random juxtaposing. Still a pose, no?

In 1975 Steve McCaffery, in a critique of my book *Pictograms from the Interior of* BC, troubled my "transcreation" of Aboriginal rock paintings by citing Baudrillard's warning of "the sinister paradox of ethnology" (38). Ethnology's object, he said, by its "death by discovery," defies being taken, and "an issue at the root of ethnopoetics itself . . . [is] translation's culpability and complicity with an ethnological project to protect the dying by death" (38). So of course, Hank, we could consider the kind of juxtaposition (collage?) you are describing in Silliman's *The Alphabet* as one method of handling this issue (what McCaffery calls, in the *Pictograms*' case, an "openness to phoneticism's 'other' (image, indeterminacy, simultaneity)" (38). That is, some way for writing to undermine the "dying" in ethnology's (and tourism's) gaze of discovery.

Surely being here now (1999), wanting to be here (Southeast Asia), I'm confronted, more self-consciously than in my 1974 project with the pictographs, with a similar need, by a common yearning to consider difference and otherness alongside the danger of my own complicity as an international middle-class tourist to, as MacCannell argues, "coordinate the differentiations of the world into a single ideology . . . linked by its capacity to subordinate others to its values, industry and future designs" (13). As a poet I try to practice in the "contradiction, conflict, violence, fragmentation, discontinuity and alienation" (MacCannell 11) of differentiation by looking for ways to keep things open (and alive).

night at the Comfort Inn near Bangkok airport
checked out Sky Blue but they were full
a very rainy day in Nathon
this year they say Amazing Samui
lots of chiles but possible
to get a non-spicy soup

Useful for me how your piece on *The Alphabet* has juxtaposed itself with this trip. So thanks!

Fred

Strangle Eight

This is it, the orifice of memory, that little Zen-hole of floating meaning, the crack of empty space with no time where the fish come to die and the navel of truth a Ziggurat of erection and clitoral inversion beyond dying some old fold reassembled in as deep and dark a well on the other side of the worm hole of grand systems then some sudden chatter of the body to replace the silicon of purity with feathers.

Some things get through and when they do we see the opening. It'll close quickly enough but for a brief moment the ~~world~~ floats in replacement mode and in a passageway the rift between an ordered body and a musical body is seemingly healed. The amalgamation is in a continuum where the foreign is located.

The music for *Dead Man* is by Neil Young and, besides Young's wonderful dissonant chording on the guitar, we can hear resonating in the background, from time to time, motors (motorcycle and car?). Young inserts the noise of a motorized boundary condition as an insightful critique of a technology (America) that is "growing us to death."

Avoid running joints for they may weaken the wall. A crack is not silent.

Rooted. Held deep. And steady. Not so much sad. Troubled maybe. But beyond tragedy, frustration, protest, the bitter daily taste of the race race, the most minimal words well up, sometimes a lament, sometimes from far back the hint of a little shout, sometimes a sombre moan of recognition, naming, placing—but playing always a song, a bluesy song of little words and little noises. "[S]lender voices," Roy Miki says, "crowd into the narrow / margin of the page" (*Saving* 31).

Miki's *Saving Face* feels its world and sings from it. Not much deflection from the senses to some other self-conscious lyricism. So the image of "stone," say, is—as it is right there in the poem—word present, seen, and heard. As well "cloud," "river," "rain," "sky," "wind." Plain words that come out of the mouth in that solitary looking up from the pit of the stomach and you are confronted with the simple weather. Poem as weather report.

What matters is counting. Only what matters to the attention of, insistence of the one base tone, tonic, at the mouth, simple, repetition ("ba/ba/ba/sho"—nickles, dimes, pennies—"hard to say/hard to tell"). Such a lucid, sure use of the poem, to place the words carefully, insistently. Or to sound themselves into place ("what lies told/them to hold"—"not wise/to be apprised/in surprise/sunrise"). Intoned, just the right words for the west coast rain, today.

But blues, here, as the residue of our lives that comes to matter.

the whole web
of intricate family ties
spun off with no beginning or end
more than a matter of time (31).

Or the "hollow/pain" becomes

all hallow pain
that can't be renewed
by a drive down the street (23).

These lines are full of body ghosts that rise to the surface, to the mouth. The beautiful ten-part "sansei poem," for example, reaches back into old photograph memory and shreds away at the remnants of grandparents and the relocated generation, their "voices scatter[ed] like shadows."

Miki's poems map out his soul, soul being his own depth, not just history and memory—though all that too—with its sadnesses, but more, the weight and shape of the imprint. The book locates the geographical and spiritual particulars of dislocation and relocation, including willful fictions.

"memory dies on the prairies"
i thought that up
when i was 12 & under
the railway bridge over
the assiniboine river (34)

He was born in Manitoba, parents ("evacuees") planted in Ste. Agathe by "*the enemy/ that never was*" (37), moves to BC, lives in Japan, all quickly enough plotted in "a pre face" at the start of the book and then churned up inside the poems. These tags of place and memory, solid enough, are only the words—between the cracks the song takes shape, "the moment (later) reconstructed in a poem" (xi). That's what's important here, why these poems are stunning in how they rise above their own narratives to sing and hum. And that's what's different for these lyric poems (and different from so much of what now tries to pass itself off as lyric), the words really do fit the music; in this case a blues. As in "two powell st festival haiku":

nisei blues

"hey i've got time to burn"
leaves around us on the grass—
at last, oh at least!

festival time

internment photos
hanging on wobbly tent walls—
gusts of the camp snow (55)

The simple play and turn go hand-in-hand with the not-so-simple content and sentiment.

The "redress" section of the book was composed "in the air, on board flights for work in the redress movement, 1984–1988." The content of such an attention as redress for Japanese-Canadians spills out, however, throughout the book. Here in this section it is the "in the air" that is the partitioning factor. So we get, besides the ironic poetic documentation of the machinations of negotiating with Ottawa, "plane" poems. In the air. Accidental meetings, in-flight notes, taking off and landing, and so forth. But more important to Miki's sense of the poem, particularly the blues poem, is the fragmented reflective mind so available in the time and shape of the airplane cocoon, hours enclosed, deep into the dark and structurally essential cracks of thinking. The first part of the last poem in the book, "22 sept 88," is a good example of how such thought and language coalesce.

settle meant?

"me ant"
a state meant

mean mea me
only words

some one sd
words'll only

get us there
to here ere er

re dress
decked out

h eir
  air
  err

the future (w)ring
the present (w)ro(ugh)t
the past (w)rung (87)

These poems hum, deep down in that solitary interface where words take the place of place, where we sift through the archives of the self. Face the music. Save it.

Loose Change (A Molecular Poetics)

the of
and to a in
that it is I
for be was as

(and/or)

"Now I know I have a heart because it's broken."

"Loose change" is meant, variously, as "what's left over" (and rattling around), what you can piggy bank on, what you can spare. I'd like to set notions of the "cents" (with a "C") in writing alongside notions of aggregation and difference. A "Molecular Poetics" would be, then, a set of tools in writing that amplify the minute and particular, the discernment of cells in composition that indicate a potential for presence, residue, evidence. Or, like the Tin Man's "Now I know I have a Heart because it's broken," now we know we're reading *writing,* writing (as opposed to some confessional realism) because its language is in pieces. Words as Cents. Histology, the study of (word) cells. The *punctum*, the beat, the gap, the gasp, the pulp, the pulse, the sigh, the sign.

As writers, some of us have attempted to upset textual transparency through the use of any heterocellular aftershock we can lay our hands on. Even silence, for example, can sometimes bring the language to the surface of a text because of the excessive noise cessation makes. But anything in language or its action that is dysmorphic can work against reading's vested interests in a coherence of form and meaning, reading's preferred attention to the words as symbols and connotations rather than, as Maurice Blanchot says,

> *Nonunifying words which would accept not to be a gateway or bridge* (pont)*, which do not "pontificate," words able to cross both sides of the abyss without filling it in and without reuniting the sides (without reference to unity) (46).*

It is at these points (not *ponts*) and recognizable gaps, where, Blanchot continues, our "waiting assures not only the beautiful hiatus that prepares the poetic act, but also and at the same time, other forms of cessation . . . and always such that the distinctions one can make between them do not avoid but solicit ambiguity" (47). Writing needs waiting. Writing needs to stop itself to know what's possible, impossible, to get within the silence of waiting.

You should sit on a log in order to hear yourself think, in order to contemplate how lost you are. The gap that interruption condenses reveals molecular alphabets necessary to proceed and recover the terrain. Here's how I put it in *Alley Alley Home Free:*

*To say: "I don't understand what this means," is, at least, to recognize that "this" means. The problem is that meaning is not a totality of sameness and predictability (**but a totality of difference and surprise**). Within each word, each sentence, meaning has slipped a little out of sight and all we have are traces, shadows, still warm ashes. The meaning available from language (**when one writes it**) goes beyond the actual instance of this word, that word. A text is a place where a labyrinth of continually revealing meanings are available (**interdependently**), a place that offers more possibility than we can be sure we know, sometimes more than we want to know. It isn't a container, static and apparent. Rather, it is noisy, frequently illegible. ~~Reading~~ (**Writing**) into meaning starts with a questioning glance, a seemingly obvious doubloon on a mast. The multiplicity can be read, should be read, even performed. But then again, perhaps meaning is intransitive and unreadable, only meant to be made. No sooner do we name meaning than it dissipates. As a sure thing, it eludes us. It arouses us to attempt an understanding, to interpret. But this is usually unsatisfying since whatever direction we* *approach from only leads us to suspect there is no one direction. No single meaning is the right one because no "right ones" stand still long enough to get caught. But because we do not know does not mean we are lost. Something that is strangely familiar, not quite what we expect, but familiar, is present. That quick little gasp in the daydream, a sudden sigh of recognition, a little sock of baby breath. Writing into meaning starts at the white page, nothing but intention. This initial blinding clarity needs to be disrupted before we're tricked into settling for a staged and diluted paradigm of the "real," the good old familiar, inherited, understandable, unmistakable lucidity of phrase that feels safe and sure, a simple sentence, just-like-the-last-time-sentence. One makes (the) difference. Meaning generates and amplifies itself, beyond itself, but never forgets; fragments of its memory and its potency exceed themselves with meaning full of desire and can only be found hiding between the words and lines (5–6; parentheses, bold face, and cross-through added).*

Further, I can see meaning, as Bruce Andrews does, as a material totality that *isn't just a negative restrictive thing, or some deterministic program. It's also something that's reproduced by action within a system and . . . a source . . . of something like what Foucault calls "positive power." The social rules that are involved in it are positive, enabling, constructive, and constitutive (53).*

In other words, I consider molecular poetics as having both social consequence and social responsibility. It all adds up. Piggy-bank poetics. A writing that wants to include the change in the total price as a way of recuperating the excess beyond consumption for a face-to-face repatterning of restricted economies.

Those little words that I'm posing as a poem called "Loose Change" at the top of this essay are the fourteen most frequently used English words as determined by a 1918 survey by Godfrey Dewey, son of Melville Dewey who devised the Dewey Decimal System. And "The" apparently occurred twice as often as anything else (Kenner 97). I immediately think of Louis Zukofsky's "Poem Beginning 'The'" (*All* 11) and his big forty-year-long personal epic poem *A*. Or Barry McKinnon's *The the*.

These little words are workers. They are part of what William Carlos Williams, in a letter to Louis Zukofsky, called "Actual word stuff, not thoughts for thoughts" (cited in Quartermain 90). Most of them are not nouns (except as syntax might make them, when faked as in the above poem).

But "Forget grammar and think about potatoes" (1975, 109), Gertrude Stein suggested in 1931. Think about words as a kind of Derridean dietary supplement.

ROAST POTATOES

Roast potatoes for (Stein 1914, 51)

Stein inserts the preposition "for" into a syntactic and poetic site that suddenly multiplies its productive possibilities in at least five ways: its aural ambiguity, ever-present within the written homophony, allows the preposition to be heard as the number noun "four"; it shifts the power to control the sentence away from "Roast potatoes" as the syntactic subject; it increases the morphemic value of "for" to a verb; it leverages into perception not only the sentence as an incomplete thought but the autonomous and infinite silence of the period; it activates the ambiguity available between "Roast" as adjective and "Roast" as verb; and the period, under this extreme pressure, is suddenly forced into motion and translates into a question mark (why, what, when, who). Suddenly the potent particularity of this preposition, its ability to perform, implodes, breaking up the transparent syntax easy reading allows.

The particular attention to the plasticity of language by Williams, Zukofsky, and Stein has been well documented by writers for whom English is a second language to the imperializing dominance of British English.[1] Stein spent her first six

[1] See Peter Quartermain's "Actual Word Stuff, Not Thoughts for Thoughts," in *Disjunctive Poetics: From Gertrude Stein and Louis*

years in Vienna and Paris, probably speaking German first, then most of her adult life in Paris speaking French and writing English. Zukofsky grew up in a Yiddish-speaking New York neighbourhood. And Williams learned Spanish and English simultaneously. The familiar "So much depends upon" of Williams' "Red Wheelbarrow" flags both the poignant necessity of objects ("so much depends upon *things*") over symbols as well as the social praxis sought after through the poetics I'm discussing here. There is an immense difference between Eliot's connotative, symbolic, and culturally inscribing "multifoleate rose" in "The Hollow Men" and the dissipating and liminal roses of Stein's rose-gram. That difference has remained apparent, though sometimes only representationally, throughout the poetics and politics of this century.

Robert Creeley, for instance, chose, out of some avowedly New England class consciousness, a much more contentious kind of poetry than, say, Robert Lowell. Creeley is a virtuoso poet of the little word and the little poem. One of his small poems in a small book called *Places* (published by a "small

---

Zukofsky to Susan Howe (90–103). See also Charles Bernstein's "Time Out of Motion," in *A Poetics* (Cambridge: Harvard University Press, 1992), 106–120. As Quartermain contextualizes this disjunctive poetics: "The situation of the American writer in the first thirty or forty years of this century bears distinct resemblances to the situation of the writer in the postcolonial world where the grand hegemonic authority of rule by imperial standard is giving way to a frequently bewildered and more often than not anarchic series of disagreements which threaten to render the social and political fabric utterly incoherent" (91).

press") pivots on a pronoun to flip back both into the poem's workings as well as into any referentiality we might have assumed and slid past:

Was

Say Mr. Snowman can
play a song for me

yes you *(n.p.)*

Creeley's recuperation of the pronoun from the normally transparent syntax of pop song is exaggerated by his twist of the verb "Was" into one of the *Places*, one of the names, titles, nouns. Verb to noun. The poem, in effect, tracks not stasis but dynamic; the words, at least there, in the poem, are not fixed but flexible. Or consider the title poem:

Places

Tidy, specific —
my head
or yours (n.p.).

The specific. And the local. Creeley notes: "No matter what becomes of it, art is local, local to a place and to a person . . . " (*Essays* 484).

Before I discuss the local as an aspect of this poetics, however, I'd like to briefly note a few more particular units of composition resulting from molecular attentions.

The social and cultural yearning for more authentic, as opposed to inherited, forms of writing runs right through from imagism and objectivism to the technologizing of the body (and thus concretizing and palpable) so typical of modernism. Williams' "a poem is a machine made of words" through Olson's "the poem must . . . be a high energy construct" (Allen 387) through Philip Whalen's "poetry is a picture or graph of the mind moving" (Allen 420) continues into Charles Bernstein's "Poetics as a sort of *applied poetic*, in the sense that engineering is a form of applied mathematics" (*Poetics* 151).

The results of technologizing the poem are intriguing and various. The objectification of the book over the past forty years is one facet. I'm thinking here of everything from Ferlinghetti's City Lights $1 Pocket Poet series to finely crafted (yet inexpensive) mimeographed books and magazines to letterpress on handmade paper earth-tone cover stock to our still-complicated fetish with "book works."

Type (*typos*) was recognized as individual. (Some of us sixties poets were trying to find our own voices as opposed, that is, to what seemed an expected and traditional meditational and cryptic "English" inner voice.) That sense of the individual imprint, outside of tradition, outside of an inherited world of form, became immediate. We used the Gestetner, the letterpress, the typewriter. Type became letter as literal and letter as object.

The alphabet. Think of, among so many, bpNichol's investment in the graphemic (what he calls "The Optophonetic Dawn" in his essay, "The "Pata of Letter Feet" (80)) throughout *The Martyrology*:

i want the world

absolute & present

all its elements

el

em

en

t's

o

pq

r

or bd

bidet

confusion of childhood's 'kaka'

the Egyptian 'KA'

soul

rising out of

the body of

the language

(*Book 4, n.p.*)

And (to just milk this quote a bit) that "body of language" in Nichol's poem comes from a substantially different (male) extrusion of anti-technology than a concurrent crucial touchstone in a feminist and sexual poetics that also seeks to conflate body and language. Nicole Brossard's

> *river moulded in the calm*
> *flood as fierce and floral fl*
> *("Articulation (sic) Deformation in Play" 63)*

posits the fragment not so much as a foregrounding of graphemic potential, as in Nichol, but as a "ritual of shock" (*Public* 13). Nichol's use of the lower-case "i" for the first-person is likewise reflexive and indicates an experiential insistence on language. What is important here is to recognize, particularly with Brossard, the sincerity and desire for social change.

> *I could perform quite well in language—you know a few tricks and you can do nice things—but I'm not interested in just performing. Because there is so much at stake for me as a woman that I want to explore and to communicate a new posture, a new perspective—and this means working with language in a way that shocks are necessary, but also memory of the body, sliding into meaning (*Politics of Poetic Form *84).*

Or, if I think back to Bruce Andrews' notion of going for the total, I might be misreading if I think of this as essentially oppositional writing. As Brossard puts it, "I am not creating an oppositional writing, I am describing a pattern that follows its course in the expression of one's identity" (*Politics of Poetic Form* 84).

Concrete (or visual) writing (along with Dada and sound, which I won't get into here) has also been an attractive form for many of these writers and the dynamics of image-text, particularly in Europe and South America, provide a structural poetics "beyond paraphrase, a poetry that often asked to be completed or activated by the reader, a poetry of direct presentation . . . using the semantic, visual, and phonetic elements of language as raw materials" (Emmett Williams vi).

One of the most serious and consequential concrete poets has been the Scots poet Ian Hamilton Finlay. Finlay has practiced concrete writing as a life writing centered in his poetry garden, "Little Sparta," south of Edinburgh. He has spent the past thirty years installing words as three-dimensional aura, sculpted text, on four-and-a-half acres of sheep-ringed Scottish hillside. Tree, bush, stone, and word come together into a *gesamtkunstwerk* of classical and neoclassical allegory and metaphor tweaked into our own paradoxical complicities with a savagery that is definitely not "noble." Climbing over a stile faced with the text "Thesis fence Antithesis gate," I am stopped suddenly in the midst of my own assumptions about fences and language. Finlay's attention to the plasticity of words is a good example of the resonating and auratic possibilities available through a poetics of the specific, minute, and particular.

But back to page text. Much that has led to a recognition of the materiality of the signifier (free verse, the breath line, shifting margins, voice, improvisation, and so forth) depends on the work done around the juncture—the space, gap, abyss, hiatus between words, before and after words, and under and over words. The democratization of verse into poetry (and lately of poetry into prose) has been sustained by attention to that site and the multiple evidence of form located there. For many writers this has meant, simply, some astute awareness of pitch, stress, and juncture. Others have felt obliged to make compositional decisions aimed at undercutting the transparency and predictability of traditional notation. For many of us, our writing lives have been largely devoted to notating the voice (after we found it, to be sure). But the juncture is also seen, variously, as regulatory and interruptive, as containing and open, as silence and noise. bpNichol chose to not use punctuation in *The Martyrology* (just as he chose to write a novel with no pronouns) as a way of contesting the closure of inherited notation. Silence as pulse, without connotation. Not silence as absence, but, as Blanchot (and John Cage) suggests, silence as transformative, again, liminal.

> *Now to this hiatus—to the strangeness, the infinite between us—there corresponds, in language, the interruption that introduces waiting. Only let it be clear that this stop is represented not necessarily or simply by silence, a blank, or a void (how crude that would be), but by a change*

in the form or the structure of language (when speaking is primarily writing) . . . (46).

That loose change rattling around in the gap includes the *punct* (perhaps not unrelated to Barthes' notion of the *punctum* in photography, that liminal spot in a photograph that is off to one side, that mysteriously appeals and shimmers the photo into something more than it seems; a kind of *ostranenie*, I suppose). Note the recognizable plasticity Steve McCaffery plays with in a chunk of *Evoba*, one of his most "molecular" expeditions.[2]

a spell.
a sphere.
a star.

a table,
a taste,
a tautology

a telegram;
a tendency;
a tension;
the microscope:
some milk   :
a mistake   :

---

[2] I touch on the environment of the hyphen in "Half-Bred Poetics" and I mention the potency of the period in "The Poetics of the Potent."

if i say, but
if he says

we might be

alluding

this. and. this. . . . and. this (78–79).

The spaces here seem to implode into strangely juxtaposed meanings. Though the shape of the poetry offers easy entertainment of the paradigmatic, the suffixing of punctuation to these triads catches attention, and the colon in "the microscope:" stanza changes expected patterning. The discursive difference between the cascading cadence of voice (in this selection) is unsettled or deflected by those colons; they shift poetic value away from stanza and cadence to just the kind of interruption and waiting Blanchot refers to. A change in reading has occurred; the "loose change" of punctuation has reoriented the textual interface to a more comprehensive terrain.

The so-called "infinite between us" mentioned in the quote from Blanchot above is also the disputed space of race. Nathaniel Mackey, in an essay titled "Other: From Noun to Verb," utilizes Amiri Baraka's way of describing white appropriation of black music, "Swing—From Verb to Noun" ("the 'noun,' [swing, jazz] white commodification, obscures or 'disappears' the 'verb' it rips off, black agency, black authority, black invention") by re-visioning the dynamic of "other" as the most recent container of difference provided by white hegemony. "Artistic othering," he advises, "has to do with innovation, invention, and change, upon which cultural health and diversity depend and thrive. Social othering has to do with power, exclusion, and privilege, the centralizing of a norm against which otherness is measured, meted out, marginalized." Mackey's "focus is the practice of the former by people subjected to the latter" (265–266). In this context, we might note such recent slippages, however slight, as Marlene Nourbese Philip's ironic shuffling of the letters of "silence" in her *Looking for Livingstone*; "Asiancy" (the title of an essay by Roy Miki in *Broken Entries*); "Ms. Edge Innate" (an essay by Camille Hernandez-Ramdwar); "e face" (the title of a poem by Mark Nakada); *Loveruage* (the title of a book by Ashok Mathur); and so forth.

I'd like to, finally, come back to some of the social action of a molecular poetics that can be enabled through that "local" Creeley hints at above. The "local," as it becomes useful and, in Rey Chow's view in her book, *Writing Diaspora*, necessary to a feminist poetics, demonstrates a crucial attention to a political negotiation with inherited structures. Chow argues that feminists, forever vigilant about how they have been constructed as "social objects," refuse "to give up the local as a base, a war front" (70). Thus, "feminine specificity" becomes necessary to those who would trouble the neutralizing postmodernist stadium of "packaging" difference, or to those who would, with Nancy Shaw, explore "the government of the eye or the rule of the gaze" (*Writing from the New Coast* 90). Further, Chow points out, the enactment of the feminist local tends to be coalitional and not just oppositional. This perhaps elucidates Brossard's anti-oppositional stance cited above. In other words, a feminist writer might use a molecular poetics both to intervent her complicity and intersubjectivity (she recognizes the containment of herself as "social object" at the same time she realizes that is a "self" she can act from) as well as to condition a productive coalition with the "government."

In her "Preface" to *Sunday Water: Thirteen Anti-Ghazals*, Phyllis Webb explains her insistence on the local and particular as a way of defying generalizing tradition.

> *"Drunken and amatory" with a "clandestine order," the subject of the traditional Ghazal was love, the Beloved representing not a particular woman but an idealized and universal image of Love ...*
>
> *Mine tend toward the particular, the local, the dialectical, and private. There are even a few little jokes. Hence "anti-Ghazals" (n.p.).*

The particular and local, in contrast to the idealized and universal, is what's needed to shift the historical (the histological). Webb's intrusion into literary form (one might argue, even into cultural hegemony and canonization) with her own feminist specificity, therefore also becomes a artful intrusion into social form in the desire to illuminate the total potential. Her "coalition" with this form is even more playful in her subsequent collection of ghazals, *Water and Light: Ghazals and Anti-Ghazals*, where the formal distinctions become so blurred I can't be sure whether I'm reading ghazal or anti-ghazal.

Lyn Hejinian's poetic sequence, *The Cell*, demonstrates a molecular poetics that is relentless and engaging in its "exploration of the relation of the self to the world, of the objective 'person' to the subjective being 'as private as my arm' . . . 'the Cell' of this work connotes several things, some contradictory: biological life, imprisonment, closure, and circulation" (jacket). The poems move by a balancing series of syntagmatic phrasings aimed at enacting the self. Her desire is to write a poem "which would not be about a person but which would be like a person . . . which [is] to its language what a person is to its landscape . . . [a poem that] would be both in language and a consequence of language and [that] would be both identifiable (or real) and interpretable (or readable)" (*Poetics Journal* 167). In other words, she wishes to locate the particularity of the selves in the particularity of language because, as she implies, "[i]t is here that the epistemological nightmare of the solipsistic self breaks down, and the essentialist yearning after truth and origin is discarded in favor of the experience of experience" (*Poetics Journal* 167). The following selection from a poem in *The Cell* illustrates how the performance of severed syntax can pressure the reorganization of thought *about* and presence *in* moments of "being":

This egg is an emotion
The sensing of a large
          amorous aptness

It is putting us in
mind of the other things
of most thoughts
Is "it" pleasure?
Endless it
And in defense of our
sex

. . .

Meanwhile, everyday life requires common
sense insatiability
A disappearance from history
Thus the breasts are two
entirely different thoughts
One is of tropical birds
and the other of the
Fire Department
Or one is of self-portraiture
and the other of new
tires
Thinking is a pleasant incorporation
It is an emotion of
sex where it resembles the
patience to travel (141–142)

The "it" of the first stanza is so released from its usual transparency that, in the last stanza, "it" becomes nominative and we can substitute "it" for "thought." Likewise, "egg," "thoughts," "breasts," "tropical birds," and "Fire Department" are released from their normally metaphorical image construct and accrue value as more equal constituents of the poetic construction as well as, because the poem is a descriptive gesture, possible facts of the self. The facts speak for themselves.

Nancy Shaw's book, *Scoptocratic*, along with her explanatory letter/statement about the book, provides a useful, creative, and critical field that reflects what I'm trying to outline. I don't want to oversimplify the range of writing that Shaw activates in this book (it is magnetic in its variety and innovation). But her compositional premise of the writing, "to mess up dominant meaning" by gazing through the "hidden and invisible spaces camouflaged as important sites of hegemonic description" in post-war Hollywood melodrama, delightfully manifests how, for this feminist writer, the infiltration by the "specific" into the total (and totalizing) "allows for a mobility that generates new discursive positions while rigorously contesting hegemonic inscription" ("Untitled" 89). "By inhabiting nodes of excess," she explains,

> *I hope to enact a poetic arrest. This is the method that I liken to my photographic examination of cinematic frames. In so doing, I attempt to accumulate a litany of all that changes from one frame to the next, thereby*

> *illuminating the most minor details crucial to the seamless constructions of such stories ("Untitled" 88).*

One example of this "poetic arrest" (from a section of *Scoptocratic* entitled "It's always the good swimmer who drowns") torques the conjunction "that" as an item normally expelled by narrative (both syntactically and cinematically):

> *One false move.*
>
> *Rumour. Scandal. Passion.*
>
> *That he became her bodyguard. I have watched you discreetly. One may infer from this episode and begin to take an interest in nature. Ascertaining all her habits. And so on. That the father met the daughter in the company of a lady (86).*

What's arrested here, among other things, is a poetic narrative that vectors back into the liminal loose change that narrative closure usually discards as excessive.

Now I know I have a heart because it's broken but should I fix it now to keep it strokin' or should I hear each piece as it is spoken and stoke heart's heat so hot I smell it smokin' or could this clock made up of parts be jokin' that missing spark a mis-read gap provokin' and little sock of baby breath not chokin' the piggy bank of words much more than tokens not just the gossip love is always cloaked in nor all the meaning text is usually soaked in but roast potatoes for a tender button so much depends upon the things unspoken and if the heart is just this clock around which clusters all that's not and if the of and to an in that it is I for be was as can set these el em en t's far apart so all the floods are fierce and floral fl's and hasten slowly stops me at my selves right now I'll have an egg because I know its yolks inside and what I have to do is crack it open.

Cat's Cradle

For myself, I realize the cradle is where I want to be. Despite the threat—and this is central to the torque of infancy—to erase temporal discriminations of difference, I *desire* the potency of training, the buzz of the tracks under the wire, the fusion of this fission, the unsettled and dissonant noise outside the hypocrisy of permanence and purity. The community of the cradle is, for me, not a lonely place to be. As I said, the homogeneous insistence of the continuous string will not contain my cradleness simply to define its own obsessions for clarity and univocal meaning, i.e., its tyrannical demand for symmetry. Patterning is multiple and I've discovered, through the elimination of the ladder, this rejection of paradigmatic experience by the young (but not only the young: 'urban Indians' and Asian tourists, skinheads, and family breadwinners alike are affiliated) a kind of coalition of free-floaters, those of us who wish to cross over on the opposite side once in awhile, is possible. And we are not like those cartoon characters of our childhood who can walk on thin air as long as they don't notice it; falling is necessary for dexterity. Both infancy and history have insisted, through the hierarchies of a knotted string, on the dynamics of improvisation—how to fake it, how to make it up. Allies in this configuration of the gap have been artists, carpenters, and fishermen—taut and loose—who, for their own reasons, have also occupied this disturbed and disturbing site. Through a substantial psychic reality of desiring objects, I long ago felt the need to contest my so-called "mother cord"—its dominance, authority, power. Another important ally in disturbing the normal tightening of the reins—a sometimes disposable reflex between two intentions, pure ones at that—has been the discourse of the chalk line, a volatile and stained venue that in the last thirty years has challenged how its productive agency has only been granted, according to our neighbour Bob, through an act of colonial line-snapping. But what's certain in this rope-a-dope debate is that you can't always get it just right. The desire for the perfect simply produces another object, a fait accompli, the repetitive delirium of rusted strands of wire cable, the invisible knot in a piece of sewing thread, the tattered and exploded end of a shoelace, a cauterized umbilical cord. This is not at all a polarization. We see that the ligament, like transcendental silk, is what remains of the tension when, at the end of a long haul, it is stripped of all its strength and fibre. The nexus of this spiritual experience of the line as a trace of thought has been described by an Arab mystic, Al-Ibn: 'the string is the string, nothing else; the string is the string, all of it . . . the string is the pure subject of the verb.' Framing the cradle does not mean that you can't read it. The sub-muscularization of the braid seems to be as caught within the progressive dynamic of Tourette's Syndrome where motion and action by a sort of sensorimotor mimicry involves, in the words of Giorgio Agamben, "a staggering proliferation of tics, involuntary spasms and mannerisms that can be defined only as a generalized catastrophe of the gestural sphere" (*Infancy and History* 136). This string is no cyborgian extension of the body. It is itself, its own nervous system allowed talking back through the permutations of an ever transmorphic screensaver. Metaphor is not easy to come by in describing this locus: binding twine, floss, packthread, leader, hamstring, lace, and so forth. Caught in the Velcro. Catgut is tempting as a forceful interpellation. But who will answer? We can find no spider's ethic here. What is held by the two hands is not meant to measure, particularly the fingers. I think we need to get wounded, down to the nemo-fibres, the ciliolum, the yarn, the thong, the rigging, the ribbon, the bandage. Yes, the wound. The interstitial space of a stage, a balcony, the trace, finally of a scar that has borrowed its outline from an imprint of the domestic. This is a track, for me, not to the realm of the spiritual (what an illusion) but to an inheritance heretofore stifled by the intentions of sacred or economic models. I want to be free to use the crumbs and scraps for the crumbness and scrapness in them, for nothing else. Time is, etymologically, according to Heraclitus, "a child playing with dice." If this is true, that is, if this is true for the cat's cradle (and mine), that string is a yoke to the spinal marrow, to the breath, to the body and its threaded thought. I want to be there in the heat of their trans-crossing, why not, through the residue of m

Bibliography

Agamben, Giorgio. *The Coming Community*. Trans. Michael Hardt. Minneapolis, U of Minnesota P, 1993.

Allen, Donald M., ed. *The New American Poetry*. New York: Grove P, 1960.

Altieri, Charles. *Enlarging the Temple: New Directions in American Poetry During the 1960s*. Lewisburg: Bucknell UP, 1979.

Andrews, Bruce. "Total Equals What: Poetics and Praxis." *Poetics Journal*, 6 (1986): 48–61.

Anzaldua, Gloria. *Borderlands La Frontera: The New Mestiza*. San Francisco: Aunt Lute Books, 1987.

Armantrout, Rae. "Poetic Silence." *Writing/Talks*. Bob Perelman, ed. Carbondale: Southern Illinois UP, 1985: 31–47. Also published as "Silence," *Poetics Journal*, 3 (May 1983): 29–32.

Arnason, David. "War Journals: A Meditation," *Border Crossings*, 10, 2 (April 1991): 9–14.

Atwood, Margaret. "Afterword" *The Journals of Susanna Moodie*. Toronto: Oxford UP, 1970: 64.

Bak, Louise. *Gingko Kitchen*. Toronto: Coach House P, 1997.

Baker, Marie Annharte. "Raced Out to Write This Up." *Secrets From The Orange Couch*, 3: 1 (April 1990): 1.

Bannerji, Himani. "Apart–hate." In McGifford: 13–15.

Barbour, Douglas. "Lyric/Anti–Lyric: Some Notes About a Concept." *Line*, 3, (Spring 1984): 45–63.

Barthes, Roland. *Writing Degree Zero*. Trans. Annette Lavers and Colin Smith. New York: Hill and Wang, 1968.

Bernstein, Charles. *Content's Dream*. Los Angeles: Sun and Moon P, 1986.

_____"Optimism and Critical Excess (Process)." In *A Poetics*. Cambridge: Harvard UP, 1992: 150–178.

Beaulieu, Michel. "La Poésie en 1980." *la Nouvelle Barre du jour* 92–93, June 1980): 8–9. Cited in Louise Dupré, "Poetry Returns to Love." *Ellipse*, 39 (1988:) 11.

Bhabha, Homi K. "Signs Taken for Wonders." In *Race, Writing, and Difference*. Henry Louis Gates Jr., ed. Chicago: U of Chicago P, 1986: 163–184.

Bhatt, Sujata. *Brunizem*. Manchester: Carcanet, 1988.

Blake, William. *Poetry and Prose of William Blake*. Geoffrey Keynes, ed. London: The Nonesuch Library, 1961.

Blanchot, Maurice. "Interruptions." Trans. Rosemarie Waldrop and Paul Auster. *The Sin of the Book*. Eric Gould, ed. Lincoln: U of Nebraska P, 1985: 43-54

Bowering, George. *The Kerrisdale Elegies*. Toronto: Coach House P, 1983.

_____"Western Writing." *Brick*, 27 (Spring 1986): 17–18.

_____"The Power is There." *The Capilano Review*, 2/2 (Spring 1990): 101–102.

_____*Errata*. Red Deer: Red Deer College P, 1988.

Brand, Dionne. *No Language is Neutral*. Toronto: Coach House P, 1990.

_____"Who Can Speak for Whom?" *Brick*, 46 (Summer 1993): 13–20.

Brossard, Nicole. *Daydream Mechanics*. Trans. Larry Shouldice. Toronto: Coach House P, 1980.

_____*The Aerial Letter*. Trans. Marlene Wildeman. Toronto: Women's P, 1988.

_____"Corps D'Energie/Rituels D'Écriture." *Public 3* (1989): 7–14.

_____"Poetic Politics." *The Politics of Poetic Form*. ed. Charles Bernstein. New York, Roof P, 1990: 73-86.

_____*Picture Theory*. Trans. Barbara Goddard. Montreal: Guernica, 1991.

Burke, Carolyn. "Without Commas: Gertrude Stein and Mina Loy." *Poetics Journal*, 4 (May 1984): 43–52.

Butler, Judith. *Excitable Speech*. New York and London: Routledge, 1997.

_____*The Psychic Life of Power*. Stanford: Stanford UP, 1997.

Callaghan, Barry. "The Impassioned Exile of Barry Callaghan." Interview with Roger Burford Mason. *Books in Canada*, XXII, 5 (Summer 1993): 9–13.

Camper, Carol, ed. *Miscegenation Blues: Voices of Mixed Race Women*. Toronto: Sister Vision, 1994.

Cha, Theresa Hak Kyung. *Dictee*. New York: Tanam P, 1982.

Chambers, Iain. *Migrancy, Culture, Identity*. London: Routledge, 1994.

Chan, Jeffery Paul, Frank Chin, Lawson Fusao Inada, and Shawn Wong, eds. *The Big Aiiieeee*! New York: Meridian, 1991.

Chang, Elaine K. "A Not-So-New Spelling of My Name: Notes Toward (and Against) a Politics of Equivocation." In

Displacements: Cultural Identities in Question. Angelika Bammer, ed. Bloomington and Indianapolis: Indiana UP, 1994: 251–266.

Chow, Rey. *Writing Diaspora: Tactics of Intervention in Contemporary Cultural Studies*. Bloomington: Indiana UP, 1993.

Clark, John. *From Feathers to Iron: A Concourse of World Poetics*. San Francisco: Tombouctou/Convivio, 1987.

Creeley, Robert. *Windows*. New York: New Directions, 1990.

_____*Places*. Buffalo: Shuffaloff P, 1990.

_____*Windows*. New York: New Directions, 1990.

Curtis, Edward S. *Portraits from North American Indian Life*. Introductions by A. D. Coleman and T. C. McLuhan. New York; Promontory P, 1972.

de Kerckhove, Derrick. *The Skin of Culture: Investigating the New Electronic Reality*. Christopher Dewdney, ed. Toronto: Sommerville House, 1995.

Deleuze, Gilles and Felix Guattari. *A Thousand Plateaus*. Minneapolis: U of Minnesota P, 1987.

_____"What is Minor Literature?" *Out There: Marginalization and Contemporary Cultures*. Martha Gever Russell Ferguson, Trinh T. Minh-ha, and Cornel West, eds. New York, Cambridge, Mass.: New Museum of Contemporary Art, MIT P, 1990: 59-70.

Derksen, Jeff. "Making Race Opaque: Fred Wah's Poetics of Opposition and Differentiation." *West Coast Line*, 18. 29, 3, (Winter 1995–96): 63–76.

Derrida, Jacques. *Dissemination*. Trans. Barbara Johnson. Chicago: U of Chicago P, 1981.

Dumont, Marilyn. *A Really Good Brown Girl*. London, Ontario: Brick, 1996.

Dyck, E. F. "The Place of Recursion in Poetry." *Brick*, 14 (Winter 1982): 20–23.

Fanon, Frantz. *Toward the African Revolution*. Trans. Haakon Chevalier. Harmondsworth: Penguin, 1967.

_____*The Wretched of the Earth*. Trans. Constance Farrington. Harmondsworth: Penguin, 1969.

Fawcett, Brian. *Cambodia; A Book for People Who Find Television Too Slow*. Vancouver: Talonbooks, 1986.

_____*Public Eye: An Investigation into the Disappearance of the World*. Toronto: HarperCollins, 1990.

Fireweed. A special issue on Asian Canadian Women, 30 (Spring 1990).

Giroux, Henry A. and Peter McLaren, eds. *Between Borders: Pedagogy and the Politics of Cultural Studies.* New York: Routledge, 1994.

Godard, Barbara. "The Discourse of the Other: Canadian Literature and the Question of Ethnicity." *The Massachusetts Review,* XXXI, 1&2 (Spring–Summer 1990): 153–184.

Goto, Hiromi. "The Body Politic." *Colour. An Issue. West Coast Line,* 28, 1–2 (1994): 218–221.

Grace, Sherrill. "Listen to the Voice: Dialogism and the Canadian Novel." In John Moss, ed., *Future Indicative.* Ottawa: U of Ottawa P, 1987): 117–136.

Grosz, Elizabeth. *Volatile Bodies: Toward a Corporeal Feminism.* Bloomington: Indiana UP, 1994.

Gunnars, Kristjana. *Carnival of Longing.* Winnipeg: Turnstone P, 1989.

Hahn, Kimiko. *The Unbearable Heart.* New York: Kaya Production, 1995.

Hancock, Geoff, ed. *Singularities: Fragments, Parafictions, Prose Poems—New Directions in Fiction and Physic.* Windsor: Black Moss P, 1990.

Harris, Claire. *The Conception of Winter.* Stratford: Williams-Wallace, 1989.

Hassan, Jamelie and Jamila Ismail. *Jamelie•Jamila Project: a collaborative bookwork.* Vancouver: Presentation House Gallery, 1992.

Hawken, Paul. Cited in Wayne Elwood, "The Global Economy." In *The New Internationalist.* April 1996: 8.

Hejinian, Lyn. "Strangeness." *Poetics Journal,* 8 (1989): 32–45.

_____"The Person and Description." *Poetics Journal,* 9 (1991): 166–170.

_____*The Cell.* Los Angeles: Sun and Moon P, 1992.

Hollander, Benjamin. "In the Extreme of Translation." *Raddle Moon,* 10. 5, 2, (Winter 1991): 34–56.

Huang, Yunte. "The Translator's Invisible Hand: The Problems in the Introduction of Contemporary Chinese Poetry." *River City,* 16, 1 (Winter 1996): 68–82.

_____"Commentary." *Rif/t* http://epc.buffalo.edu/ 4.1 (Spring 1995): n.p.

Hutcheon, Linda and Marion Richmond, eds. *Other Solitudes: Canadian Multicultural Fictions.* Toronto: Oxford UP, 1990.

Inada, Lawson, Fusao. "On Being Asian American." In *The Big Aiiieeeee!: And Anthology of Chinese American and Japanese American Literature*. eds. Jeffery Paul Chan, Frank Chin, Lawson Fusao Inada, and Shawn Wong. New York: Penguin Books, 1991: 619.

Ismail, Jam. *from the DICTION AIR*. Self-published, n.d.

_____*Sexions*. Self-published. Kitsilano, Vancouver, 1984.

_____"(Translit)." *West Coast Line* 30.21, 3 (1997): 46–58.

_____"Scared Texts." In *Many-mouthed Birds*. Bennett Lee and Jim Wong-Chu. eds. Vancouver: Douglas & McIntyre, 1991: 124–135.

Kearns, Lionel. *Convergences*. Toronto: Coach House P, 1983.

Keats, John. *The Selected Letters of John Keats*. ed. Lionel Trilling. New York: Doubleday, 1951.

Kenner, Hugh. "Oppen: The Little Words." *Scripsi*, 6, 1 (1990): 97–108.

Kim, Myung Mi. *Under Flag*. San Francisco: Kelsey Street P, 1991.

Kipnis, Laura. "Aesthetics and Foreign Policy." In *Ecstasy Unlimited: On Sex, Capital, Gender, and Aesthetics*. Minneapolis: U of Minnesota P, 1993: 207–218.

Kiyooka, Roy. "One Signature: *Kumo/Cloud/s & Sundry Pieces*." *West Coast Line*, 24. 3 (Winter 1990): 97–128.

_____"We Asian North Americanos: An unhistorical 'take' on growing up yellow in a white world." *West Coast Line*, 24-3 (Winter 1990): n.p.

_____"A February Postscript: to October's Piebald Skies & Other Lacunae." *Pacific Windows*. ed. Roy Miki. Vancouver: Talonbooks, 1997: 291-296

Kostash, Myrna. "Pens of Many Colours." *The Canadian Forum*, June 1990: 17–19.

Krauss, Rosalind. "The Im/Pulse to See." In *Vision and Visuality*. ed. Hal Foster. Seattle: Bay P, 1988: 51–78.

Kroetsch, Robert. *The Sad Phoenician*. Toronto: Coach House P, 1979.

_____"For Play and Entrance: The Contemporary Canadian Long Poem." *Open Letter*, 5/4 (Spring 1983): 91–110.

_____"The Frankfurt Hauptbanhoff." *Open Letter*, 5/7 (Spring 1984): 83–93.

Ladha, Yasmin. "*Circum the Gesture*." Unpublished MA thesis. U of Calgary, 1993.

Lazer, Hank. "Education, Equality and Ethnography in Ron

Silliman's *The Alphabet*." *Quarry West* 34: 68–97.
Lee, Sky. *Disappearing Moon Cafe*. Vancouver: Douglas & McIntyre, 1990.
Levin, Samuel R. *Linguistic Structures in Poetry, Janua Linguarum* 23. The Hague: Mouton, 1964.
Lew, Walter, ed. *Premonitions: The Kaya Anthology of New Asian North American Poetry*. New York: Kaya Production, 1995.
Lippard, Lucy R. *Mixed Blessings: New Art in a Multicultural America*. New York: Pantheon Books, 1990.
Lowry, Malcolm. *Under the Volcano*. Harmondsworth: Penguin, 1962.
Mackey, Nathaniel. "from From A Broken Bottle Traces of Perfume Still Emanate." *Code of Signals*, Michael Palmer, ed. *Io* (30, 1983): 11–21.
_____*Discrepant Engagement: Dissonance, Cross-Culturality, and Experimental Writing*. Vol. 71 of Cambridge Studies in American LIterature and Culture. Cambridge: Cambridge UP, 1993.
Maclear, Kyo. "The Walls Between Us Are Paper Thin." *Colour. An Issue. West Coast Line*, 28. 1-2 (1994): 222–225.
MacLeod, Kathryn. *How Two*. Vancouver: Tsunami Editions, 1987.
Mandel, Eli. "The Ethnic Voice in Canadian Writing." In Diane Bessai and David Jackel, eds. *Figures in a Ground*. Saskatoon: Western Producer Prairie Books, 1978: 264–277.
Maracle, Lee. "Trickster Alive and Crowing." *Fuse*, xiii, 1&2 (Fall 1989): 29–31.
Marie Baker. "Raced Out to Write this Up," *Secrets from the Orange Couch*, 3, 1 (April 1990): 1.
Marlatt, Daphne. "Given This Body." An interview by George Bowering. *Open Letter*, 4/3 (Spring 1979): 33–88.
_____"In the Month of Hungry Ghosts." *The Capilano Review*, 16/17 (1979): 45–95.
_____"Musing With Mothertongue." *Tessera* 1/*Room of One's Own* 8, 4, (January 1984): 53–56. Also in her *Readings from the Labyrinth*. Edmonton: NeWest Press, 1998: 9-14.
_____"Vers-ions Con-Verse: A Sequence of Translations" (Susan Knutson, Kathy Mezei, Daphne Marlatt, Barbara Godard, Gail Scott). *Tessera*, 6 (Spring 1989): 16–23.
_____*Salvage*. Red Deer: Red Deer College P, 1991.
McCaffery, Steve. "Anti-Phonies: Fred Wah's *Pictograms from the Interior of* BC," *North of Intention: Critical Writings*

1973–1986. Toronto and New York: Nightwood Editions/Roof Books, 1986: 30–38.
_____"The Death of the Subject: The Implications of Counter-Communication in Recent Language-Centered Writing." *Open Letter,* 3/7 (Summer 1977): 61–77.
_____*Evoba*. Toronto: Coach House P, 1987.
_____"In Ten$^{t}{}_{s}$ion: Dialoguing with bp." *Tracing the Paths: Reading & Writing the Martyrology.* ed. Roy Miki. Vancouver: Talonbooks/Line, 1988: 72–94.
_____"Charles Olson's Art of Language: The Mayan Stratum in Projective Verse." *Ellipsis,* (Spring 1990): 37–47.
_____Presentation on bpNichol at the Simon Fraser University Special Collections, September 24, 1998.
MacCannell, Dean. *The Tourist: A New Theory of the Leisure Class*. New York: Schocken Books, 1976.
McFarlane, Scott. "Act Three: Museum Culture: An International Scene from a Sansei Melodrama." *The Skin on our Tongues*. ed. Hiromi Goto-Tongu, Ashok Mathur, and Suzette Mayr. Calgary: A special issue of *absinthe* (1993): 46–48.
McGifford, Diane and Judith Kearns, eds. *Shakti's Words: And Anthology of South Asian Canadian Women's Poetry.* Toronto: TSAR, 1990.
McKinnon, Barry. *The the*. Toronto: Coach House P, 1980.
_____*Pulp Log*. Prince George: Caitlin P, 1991.
Miki, Roy and Fred Wah, eds. *Colour. An Issue. West Coast Line,* 13/14 (Spring/Fall 1994).
Miki, Roy. "Asiancy: Making Space for Asian Canadian Writing." In his *Broken Entries: Race, Subjectivity, Writing*. Toronto: The Mercury P, 1998: 101–124.
_____*Saving Face: Poems Selected 1976–1988*. Winnipeg: Turnstone P, 1991.
Minh-ha, Trinh T. *When the Moon Waxes Red: Representation, Gender, and Cultural Politics*. New York: Routledge, 1991.
Mitchell, W. J. T. "Pluralism as Dogmatism." *Critical Inquiry,* (Spring 1986): 494–502.
Mouré, Erin. *Furious*. Toronto: Anansi, 1988.
Moyes, Lianne. "Dialogizing the Monologue of History and Lyric: Lionel Kearns' Convergences." *Open Letter,* 7/5 (1989): 15–27.
Mullen, Harryette. *Muse and Drudge*. Philadelphia: Singing Horse P, 1995.
Nichol, bp. *The Martyrology Books 3 & 4*. Toronto: Coach House P, 1976.

_____*Translating Translating Apollinaire*. Milwaukee: Membrane P, 1979.

_____*The Martyrology, Book 5*. Toronto: Coach House P, 1982.

_____"The Pata of Letter Feet." *Open Letter*, 6/1 (Spring 1985): 79–95.

_____"Notebook a composition on composition." *Open Letter*, 6/2–3 (Summer–Fall 1985): 152 (and throughout issue).

_____"Syntax Equals the Body Structure." bpNichol in conversation with Daphne Marlatt and George Bowering. *Line*, 6 (Fall 1985): 21–44.

_____"In/Ov Native Writing." *American Book Review* (May–June 1988): 1, 7.

_____*Gifts: The Martyrology Book(s) 7 &*. Toronto: Coach House P, 1990: unpaginated.

Nichols, Miriam. "The Subject of Experience: Writing Beyond the Concept in the Work of bpNichol and Daphne Marlatt." Presented at the 1999 ACCUTE meeting in Sherbrooke, Québec.

Novalis. "A translation of Book IX of The Encyclopedia." Published as *Archai*. Trans. Karl Siegler. Burnaby, BC: Simon Fraser U, April 1973.

Olson, Charles. *Human Universe and Other Essays*. New York: Grove P, 1967.

_____*Archaeologist of Morning*. London: Cape Golliard P, 1970.

_____*Additional Prose: A Bibliography on America, Proprioception & Other Notes & Essays*. ed. George F. Butterick. Bolinas: Four Seasons Foundation, 1974.

_____*Muthologos: The Collected Lectures and Interviews*. Vol. 2 of 2 vols. Four Seasons Foundation, n.d.

_____*The Maximus Poems*. Berkeley: U of California P, 1983.

Ondaatje, Michael. *Running in the Family*. Toronto: McClelland & Stewart, 1982.

Oppen, George. *Collected Poems*. New York: New Directions, 1975.

Original: Chinese Language-Poetry Group. Trans. by Jeff Twitchell. Brighton: Parataxis Editions, 1994.

Pal, Rajinderpal. "apna sangeet." *The Skin on our Tongues*. ed. Hiromi Goto-Tongu, Ashok Mathur, and Suzette Mayr. Calgary: A special issue of *absinthe* (1993): 39–40.

Parameswaran, Uma. "In Our Ancestral Home." In McGifford: 66.

Perloff, Marjorie. *The Poetics of Indeterminacy* Princeton: Princeton UP, 1981.

Philip, Marlene Nourbese. "Anonymous." In *Salmon Courage* (1983). Reprinted in *Grammar of Dissent,* poetry and prose by Claire Harris, M. Nourbese Philip, and Dionne Brand. ed, Carol Morrell. Fredericton: Goose Lane Edition, 1994.

Phillips, Claire. "Violent Acts Within Public Discourse." *Poetics Journal,* 6 (1986): 46–47.

Ping, Wang. ed. *New Generation: Poems from China Today.* Minnesota Hanging Loose P, 1999.

Pound, Ezra. *ABC of Reading*. New York: New Directions, 1960.

Prairie Fire. Special issue on New Mennonite Writing. 11, 2 (Summer 1990).

Pratt, Mary Louise. *Imperial Eyes: Travel Writing and Transculturation.* London: Routledge, 1992.

_____"Yoy soy la Malinche': Chicana Writers and the Poetics of Ethnonationalism." *Twentieth-century Poetry: From Text to Context.* ed. Peter Verdonk. London: Routledge, 1993: 171–187.

Quartermain, Peter. *Disjunctive Poetics: From Gertrude Stein and Louis Zukofsky to Susan Howe.* Cambridge: Cambridge UP, 1992.

Rif/t http://epc.buffalo.edu/ 4.1 (Spring 1995): n.p.

Said, Edward. *After the Last Sky: Palestinian Lives.* New York: Pantheon, 1986.

Schwartz, Leonard. "Business as Usual: Towards a C=H=I=N=E=S=E Language Poetry?" *Talisman,* 15 (Winter 1995–96): 172–175.

Scott, Gail. "Virginia and Colette on the outside looking in." *Brick,* 28 (Fall 1986): 30–34.

_____*Spaces Like Stairs.* Toronto: The Women's P, 1989.

Shaw, Nancy. *Scoptocratic.* Toronto: ECW P, 1992.

_____"Untitled letter." *Writing from the New Coast: Technique.* ed. Peter Gizzi and Juliana Spahr. Buffalo and Stockbridge: o-blek editions and Poetics Program, 1993: 88–91.

Shikatani, Gerry. *1988.* Toronto: Aya P, 1989.

Shipley, Joseph T. *The Origins of English Words: A Discursive Distionary of Indo-European Roots.* Baltimore: The Johns Hopkins UP, 1984.

Shklovsky, Viktor. "Art as Technique." *Russian Formalist Criticism: Four Essays.* Trans. Lee T. Lemon and Marion J. Reis. Nebraska: U of Nebraska P, 1965: 3–24.

Silliman, Ron. "The New Sentence." *Hills,* 6/7 (Spring 1980): 190–217.

_____"Migratory Meaning." *Poetics Journal* 2 (September 1982): 27–41.

_____"New Prose New Prose Poem," In *Postmodern Fiction: A Bio-bibliographical Guide.* ed. Larry McCaffery. New York: Greenwood P, 1986: 157–174.

_____*The New Sentence.* New York: Roof Books, 1987.

_____"You." *CrossConnect.* http://ccat.sas.upenn.edu/xconnect, 1998.

Smith, Paul. *Discerning the Subject.* Minneapolis: U of Minnesota P, 1987.

Stein, Gertrude. *Tender Buttons.* 1914 edition reissued. Los Angeles: Sun & Moon P, 1914.

_____*How to Write.* New York: Dover, 1975.

Suknaski, Andrew. "Out of Narayan to Bifrost/the word arresting entropy." *Brick,* 14 (Winter 1982): 5–6, 11–17, 24–25, 30–31, 38–39, 44–45, 50–52, 54–56.

Sullivan, Rosemary. "Who are the immigrant writers and what have they done?" *The Globe and Mail,* October 17, 1987.

Taussig, Michael. *Mimesis and Alterity: A Particular History of the Senses.* New York and London: Routledge, 1993.

Telling It Book Collective, eds. *Telling It: Women and Language Across Cultures.* Vancouver: Press Gang, 1990.

Thorpe, Michael. "Opposition, Multicultural Apartheid or Connection?" *The Toronto South Asian Review,* 9, 1 (Summer 1990): 1–10.

van Herk, Aritha. *Places Far From Ellesmere.* Red Deer: Red Deer College P, 1990.

_____*A Frozen Tongue.* Sydney: Dangeroo P, 1992.

Venuti, Lawrence. "Translation as Cultural Politics: Regimes of Domestication in English." *Textual Practice,* 7, 2 (1993): 208–223.

Wah, Fred. *Earth.* Canton, N.Y.: Institute of Further Studies, 1974.

_____"Making Strange Poetics." *Open Letter,* 6/2–3 (1985): 213–221.

_____*Music at the Heart of Thinking.* Red Deer: Red Deer College P, 1987.

_____"Making Stranger Poetics: A Canadian Poetics (Plural) Inventory." *Span,* 31 (February 1991): 49–62.

_____*Alley Alley Home Free.* Red Deer: Red Deer College P, 1992.

_____"A Poetics of Ethnicity." *Twenty Years of Multiculturalism: Successes and Failures.* ed. Stella Hryniuk. Winnipeg: St.

John's College P, 1992: 99–110.
_____*Diamond Grill*. Edmonton: NeWest Press, 1997.
_____"High(briti)Tea Menu." In limited ed. for installation/performance with Haruko Okano. Vancouver, August 27, 1999.
Warland, Betsy. "Far As the I Can See." *Tessera,* 3 published by *Canadian Fiction Magazine,* 57 (1986): 92–96.
Watney, Simon. "Making Strange: The Shattered Mirror." *Thinking Photography*. Victor Burgin, ed. Basingstoke, England: Macmillan, 1982: 154–176.
Webb, Phyllis. *Sunday Water: Thirteen Anti-Ghazals*. Lantzville: Island Writing Series, 1982.
_____*Water and Light*. Toronto: Coach House P, 1984.
Whalen, Philip. *Memoirs of an Interglacial Age*. San Francisco: Auerhahn, 1960.
Williams, Emmett, ed. *An Anthology of Concrete Poetry*. New York: Something Else P, 1967.
Williamson, Janice. "Sounding the Difference: An Interview with Smaro Kamboureli and Lola Tostevin." *Canadian Forum,* Jan. 1987: 34.
Wong, Nellie. *Dreams in Harrison Railroad Park*. San Francisco: Kelsey St. P, 1977.
Wong, Shelley Sunn. "Unnaming the Same: Theresa Hak Kyung Cha's *Dictee*" In *Writing Self Writing Nation*. ed. Elaine H. Kim and Norma Alarcon. Berkeley: Third Woman P, 1994.
Wong-Chu, Jim. *Chinatown Ghosts*. Vancouver: Pulp P, 1986.
Wreggitt, Andrew. "The Apple Tree Goes Arga Warga or The Garden of Bloody Eden." *Event*, 19, 1 (Spring 1990): 27.
Yeh, Michelle. "The 'Cult of Poetry' in Contemporary China" In *The Journal of Asian Studies*, 55, 1 (February 1996): 51–80.
Young, Neil. "Dead Man: Music from and Inspired by the motion picture." Vapour Records, 1996.
Ziqing, Zhang, ed. *Chinese Language Poetry*. Trans. by Liu Feng. Nanjing: Nanging U, 1993.
_____and Yunte Huang. *Selected Language Poems by Charles Bernstein, Hank Lazer, James Sherry*. Chengdu: Sichuan Literature and Art Publishing House, 1993.
Zukofsky, Louis. *Prepositions*. Berkeley: U of California P, 1981.
_____*All: The Collected Short Poems 1923–1958*. New York: W. W. Norton, 1965.

Index